HASHTAGS and ZOOM Bewilder This BOOMER

Finding the Funny While Aging

MARY ANN HOYT

ISBN: 978-1-09833-567-0 (print)
ISBN: 978-1-09833-568-7 (ebook)

To my dear family

CONTENTS

Introduction

###

I'm guessing you read my first book. Those who liked it told me so. Those who didn't like it—well, all they said was, "Congratulations." In either case, you're giving me another chance. If you are worried that I have my act together by now—do not fear. Being ok with my inadequacies gives me freedom to laugh at myself and the permission to write it down.

It feels so good to sit at my computer and write again. What was I doing since my first book was published? Well, as any writer will tell you—in today's world, the process of getting your work published can be more agonizing than the pains of birthing a baby.

Never birthed a baby? Well, how about the time you lost your wallet with all your credit cards, driver's license, and your gift certificate for a Swedish massage. And then you spent hours on the phone to cancel the cards and get new ones re-issued, forgetting all your passwords in the ensuing panic.

Or—here's another one. If you are a nurse and one day at the hospital, you had to write 10 incident reports, with follow-up calls to the doctors because you forgot to give your patients their morning insulin or medications. Oh wait—that was just the nightmare I had the other night.

Anyway, like labor, I would rather think about the birth.

And when the big day came and I held my newly published book in my hands like it was the Holy Grail, I found out I needed to *sell* my book. Well, I didn't have a good feeling about that, since I had flashbacks of ringing doorbells to sell Girl Scout cookies in 1959—praying that nobody would answer the door.

So on to my daily trials and travails. Keep in mind that despite my sometimes snarky observations, I am very aware that these are all first world problems, and I am grateful for every day I get out of bed.

Reminiscing

Retirement gives you a lot of time to reminisce. I remember the day my siblings and I walked to school with umbrellas in a heavy rain. My feet couldn't escape the little rivers of water in the streets. By the time I reached my first grade classroom, Sister Agatha Marie saw my sopping wet shoes and socks, and had me take them off and put them on the radiator to dry. Sitting at my desk, I looked like a double amputee, as I curled my little legs up under the seat, sure that all 55 heads were staring at my naked feet.

I'm amazed how much more sophisticated our grandchildren are than I was at that age. I cannot, for the life of me, imagine any of our grandkids accepting the job I had in second grade, much less feeling proud of it. Back then, St Ursula's Catholic school had more than 50 kids in a classroom, and back then, everybody went to the bathroom at the same time before recess. So, 25 girls lined up for the bathroom that had five stalls. In their haste to get to recess, they either didn't flush or didn't wait till the tank filled up from the last person.

I raised my hand when the class was asked for a volunteer to go in after recess and go from toilet to toilet and flush if need be. Pathetic, right? And the next year when I moved up to third grade, I asked my new teacher if I could have my old job back, wondering why she had a bewildered look on her face. Considering my current OCD issues with public bathrooms, I have no idea why I wanted this job. Of course, maybe that job was the root of my issues.

You might be wondering why the janitor wouldn't do this. Well, this was Catholic school in the fifties. We used to clap the erasers, sweep the floors in the classroom at the end of the day, and use a dust brush to get under the desks. I guess it was a good life lesson—nobody should be above using a broom.

I was a rule following teacher's pet. But I'm sure I was also a royal pain for the young nuns who tried to teach a roomful of kids, while I raised my hand inquisitively a hundred times a day. Things haven't changed. I've just substituted Google.

Except for asking questions, I was very shy—right through third grade. I remember we had to make a poster for geography and show farm animals. I cut out pictures of cows and pasted them on a poster— black and white Holsteins and brown Jerseys. When my name was called I had to go to the front of the class, hold my poster up, and talk about the cows. I stood there staring at the class—silent.

"Mary Ann," coaxed Sister Most Holy, "would you like to tell us about your poster?"

More silence.

My shyness was not consistent. Later the same year of the missed opportunity with the cows, the teacher had to leave the room for five minutes. I got upset when all the kids started talking (a no no in Catholic school). So I walked to the front of my row of desks and started telling everyone to be quiet, (while wagging my finger) or they were going to be in real trouble. Dear God, I was weird.

Another time (actually more than once), I had incidents I attribute to either my early shyness or maybe just poor timing. We went home for lunch, and after getting back to school in the afternoon, I started to feel sick. My stomach bugs always popped up out of nowhere. Instead of telling the teacher I needed to use the bathroom because I was about to be sick, I waited until the last second, then jumped out of my seat and threw up right smack in the center of the aisle. I can only imagine the state of mind I put that nun into—55 kids and vomit in aisle 4.

I really started coming into my own in fourth grade. Or so I thought. I remember an eighth-grade boy who used to come to each classroom every Friday afternoon selling copies of the *Catholic Boy Magazine.* On one such Friday, Sister Margaret Mary was paging through a sample and said, "Oh, a very nice article about Perry Como." For those of you too young to know Perry Como, he was the '50s crooner, made famous by songs such as "Catch a Falling Star" and the Thanksgiving favorite, "Home for the Holidays." He wasn't bad looking either. So, I thought I would do a very cool teenage thing (even though I was only 10 years old). When Sister commented on him, I started to jump from my seat, sighing loudly as if I were about to faint, assuming all the other girls would do the same. Sister Margaret Mary, the eighth-grade boy, and 54 heads swung in my direction.

In my sixth-grade brain, I was destined for great things. I still find it incredible that I sang the Rodgers and Hammerstein song, "Getting to Know You" in the school talent show—all by myself.

Nursing School

###

The career trajectory in my high school psyche went from becoming a cloistered nun, to a missionary in the East Indies, to a star on Broadway—finally deciding to be the modern-day Florence Nightingale.

Nursing school back in 1968 was nerve wracking. The night before I was the student *scrub* nurse in the OR, I inhaled half of my roommate's birthday cake because I was so anxious.

As a freshman, one of our instructors terrified me because of her stern demeanor. I had the unfortunate luck of having her stand next to me, in her triple-starched white uniform, while I gave a bed shampoo to my patient, using a clumsy tray that went under her head and drained into a bucket at the side of the bed. Since I didn't put the required towel under her neck, she was lying in a pool of bubbly water by the time I was finished. I vividly remember the steely gray eyes of my instructor piercing right through me.

I also got reprimanded by another instructor, when I sent my patient to the OR for his surgery. As the gurney was wheeled down the hallway, I waved to him and yelled, "Good luck!" Apparently, when a patient is about to have his belly slit open with a knife, "good luck" is not the appropriate thing to say.

One time in nutrition class we were learning about diabetes, and for our clinical experience, we were supposed to pick a patient and give them tips on the diabetic diet. Well, when my instructor went in to speak with the patient and his daughter later that afternoon to ask them how I did, the daughter was furious because I had frightened her father. Apparently, I explained how there was a chance he could break out in a sweat and pass out if he didn't eat after he took his insulin;

and I must have been very dramatic—proudly spewing out all the medical terminology I had absorbed from my classes. The poor guy nearly passed out, and it had nothing to do with insulin.

I'll never forget my OB rotation. One day, I was assigned to stay with a woman in labor for the whole 7-3 shift. The RN on duty was the official nurse who monitored her and gave the medications. So all I did (whenever she had a strong contraction) was say, "You're doing fine. Just breathe, breathe—nice and slow." I said this multiple times during her contractions while massaging her back.

Years later, when the tables were turned and I was in labor, I thought of that sweet patient who listened to me drone on and on for eight hours, and I wondered why her foot never popped out from under the blanket to kick me in the stomach.

How I Met My Husband

###

Did I ever tell you how I met my husband? In 1969, I was a senior in my three-year hospital-based nursing program in Allentown, PA. The buzz, right before the holidays, was that a new assistant administrator was hired by the hospital's board of trustees. After seeing his picture in the newsletter, all the seniors thought he was *hot*, though I don't think that was the descriptive word back then.

Lo and behold, I walked into the nurses' library a few days later and who was sitting there but the new assistant administrator and another student a few yards away from him. She left shortly after and then my devious mind went to work.

"Mr. Hoyt, how do you like it here at our hospital?" Taken a little off guard, he responded, "Very much. Yes, I like it very much."

Thrilled that he acknowledged me, I continued, "Will you be coming to our Christmas party tonight?" Getting an affirmative answer, I felt like I was on a roll.

Since I was secretary of my class, I stood in the receiving line of our Student Nurses Christmas party at the Allentown Women's Club. As he passed me, I greeted him, took his overcoat—and hid it in the janitor's closet. I was floating that night, after he came to my non-alcoholic punch bowl. When it was time to leave, I let him flounder for a bit, as he didn't know what happened to his coat.

"Mr. Hoyt, I believe you are looking for this," I said, making sure I achieved eye contact—(which, by the way, remains a challenge to this day).

Back in my dorm room, I drove my room-mate crazy, as she was trying to study for her neurology final. "He still doesn't know my name!" After pacing for an hour, it came to me. As secretary of my class,

I just needed to send a thank-you note to acknowledge his graciousness in coming to the party. And so it began.

After we got engaged, Paul said to me, "By the way, when I mentioned to my boss how nice it was that you sent a thank-you note, on behalf of the nursing school, he told me that he never got one. In fact, he said to me that I had a very conniving nurse on my hands; and I should either run the other way, or start saving for an engagement ring."

"And who is the conniving one? You waited to tell me this until after I had the ring on my finger!"

My Mothering Mistakes

Am I the only mother who would love a do-over? Although, asking myself that question after a glass of wine is always followed by, "Am I nuts?" I'm counting on my kids to recall my recurring statement, "Mothers make mistakes. Just know that I always loved you."

Mistake #1: As I peruse through old photos, I am reminded of our past vacations to the beach in Rhode Island—our little bathing beauties with globs of white zinc oxide smeared on their blistered lips; and telling them the red color on their sun-burned shoulders would turn to tan overnight. Did I never hear of sun block in the '70s? I must have had the flu when the dermatology class was taught in my nursing school, considering how I used to sunbathe on our school's roof deck, my body covered in oil. I dread when our adult kids start going for their dermatology appointments.

Mistake #2: When visiting our grandchildren, I watch them chopping vegetables for dinner, or stirring brownie batter, and I think about how I was the kitchen czar with my own kids. I guarded my domain from eight little hands—unless I was in the frame of mind to have them make something creative for lunch that I, not company, would eat. Of course, if I made cookies, I'd give them a glob of dough to roll into little balls and dip in sugar. Other than that—not much else.

Mistake#3: Speaking of food, I expected our kids to eat everything on their plates. I remember my mother telling *me* this, because the children were starving in Europe. I switched the location of the starving children to Africa. And how again does that reasoning work to feed the world's hungry children?

Anyway, I decided I wouldn't be unreasonable like my parents, who demanded we finish the slab of liver on our plates. Instead, I insisted that Eleanor (who is now a vegetarian), eat the seven kernels of the corn that I put in her dish. Not asking too much, right? She hated corn, and didn't mind going to her room in rebellion. I am getting blamed for any food issues they now have. The seven kernels of corn were just not worth it.

I remember grocery shopping with our older two children when they were 2 years old and 11 months—and that would be Sharon, who sat in the grocery cart, and Eleanor, who was perched on my back in a papoose, which was popular in the '70s. As I approached the checkout line, they would start to get cranky, and I would pull out the "Sunbeam" white bread. Ripping up a slice, I would hand off the pieces of bread as if I were feeding ducks in a pond, as we stood waiting in line. Apparently, I started them on the carb express train back then.

Mistake #4: One of my biggest regrets stemmed from an idea my good friend had down the street. Her little kids *never* napped, so she decided to get them washed and in their pj's before dinner—easier than getting cranky, tired kids into the bathtub at 8 p.m. I thought she had a great idea, so I followed suit. Until my six-year-old was so mad at me one spring day at 5 p.m. as she heard all the other neighborhood kids riding their bikes outside, that she ran into her room and banged her little hand on the window pane, cracking the glass. She wasn't hurt, thank God, but cried because she was so startled at what she did. I was devastated. I held her in my arms and rocked her, telling her that the idea I had was a dumb idea. Yep, I've had to say "Just know that I love you," more times than I can count.

So, before I start sounding like "Mommy Dearest," let's just move along to the next chapter.

The Grateful Dead Concert

Our family loves music, but our kids tell me I must have slept through the '70s because I am clueless about the songs from that decade. They actually got the sleeping part wrong. I slept very little during the '70s. Our four babies who arrived during those years saw to that. I did hear about Woodstock, back in 1969, but that event was held during the last year of my sheltered, Catholic nursing school days, and the only thing I remember was that my younger brother was fuming because my parents wouldn't let him go.

When our kids were in high school, they wanted to go to a Grateful Dead concert at the Meadowlands, in New Jersey, about an hour from our house. Of course I said no. "Oh, but Craig will watch us."

Craig was the boyfriend of our daughter, Eleanor. After Paul and I had an emergency kitchen conference, we let the three of our oldest go. When 11:45 rolled around, Paul and I were pacing the floor. Annie, the youngest, was eaves-dropping on the steps to the second floor, enjoying every minute of the drama.

We didn't have cell phones back then, so I did what any responsible mother would do—I called the state police. "Were there any accidents at the concert, Officer?"

"Ma'am, the concert just let out 15 minutes ago, and there's a lot of traffic, so I'm sure they'll be home soon."

Craig got them home safely. He is now our son-in-law, with two teenage daughters. Ha—and I am enjoying every minute of it.

Mother of the Bride (and Groom) Hair Disasters

###

I have one bit of advice if you are going to be a "Mother of the bride, or groom." It's one of the few times in middle age when you can make a fashion statement. And the pressure's on, as you walk up the aisle, feeling a little bit like it's your own wedding.

If only then I realized, after that 30 second walk, you disappear into oblivion, with all eyes on the bride and her attendants. And let's face it, all the guests are pre-occupied with their own looks, as if they're attending the Oscars.

I also discovered it's not the gown that will make or break your 30 second image. It's the hair. With the first wedding, I had a boring hairstyle that I can't even describe. A few days before the second wedding, I had my hair cut and shaped into what I thought was a cute style. I should have known to give my hair a few weeks to get over the shearing shock of a short hairdo. Try as I might, I couldn't encourage it to grow a millimeter.

Third time around was in Pittsburgh, a few hours from our home. I made the fatal error of calling a salon I found on the Internet and scheduled an updo for my hair that was now long, two hours before the wedding. I felt the stylist tugging and pulling my hair, and most of the time she had me facing away from the mirror. I should tell you I get intimidated by hair stylists, no matter how unintimidating they are. I started holding my breath, thinking maybe this will all end right. But it didn't. When she was done I looked at the back of my head, holding a small mirror, and saw sheer beauty and artistry—my hair wound in an elegant updo twist. And then I looked, horrified, at the front—my hair pulled back severely on the sides with the top of my head as flat as a pancake. The wedding was in an hour and I panicked. If I tried to reverse this disaster, the mother of the groom would be absent from her 30 second walk up the aisle—which, by the way, was preserved forever on wedding videos.

I was lamenting afterward to a friend who said to me matter-of-factly, "Well, you've got one more wedding to get it right."

Retirement in Delaware

#

Retirement in Delaware is good. It would be even better if we lived a bit closer to the families of our four children. "Over the river and through the woods to grandmother's house we go," doesn't happen as much in today's world. As all grandparents know, the kids are tethered to their homes because of their sports schedules and creative activities—enough to fill a computer spreadsheet. So most of the time, we visit them.

And to think I felt like super mom, back in the day, because I got our kids to a weekly scout meeting and basketball game.

So far, we enjoy living in Delaware, dismissing our adult children's concerns that we are too far away for them to take care of us, should we both simultaneously collapse on the floor one day. Of course, by the time I finish this second book, we may be in a nursing home.

We decided to downsize, and live in one of the new developments where the homes have "cozier" spacing between them than I had been used to. Or should I say, since I grew up in Bethlehem, PA. Because my childhood home was a duplex, with an alleyway separating us from the next one, we had bright sunlight only in the early morning and late afternoon. My mother ensured our privacy with semi-sheer curtains, and only the tops of the windows were bare. We grew up with an appreciation of the clouds dancing across the blue sky.

I made sure our home in Delaware had lots of windows with a sunny, southwest exposure—no shades, no blinds, and no curtains during the day to block those glorious sunbeams! (And yes, we have shades in our bedroom.)

With the exception of the pine trees and tulip poplars lining the back of our yards, we have no barriers between the houses. I asked a neighbor soon after we moved in if anyone thought about shrubbery, or a fence of some kind between our back yards. She hesitated and said, "I don't think so." I guessed that was a no.

It was a little awkward, especially after we added our deck, when we sat out to have a glass of wine before dinner. "Paul, should we invite them over?" I'd ask my husband, after seeing neighbors out on their patio. Luckily, these were just growing pains. Kind of like being in sixth grade all over again.

Yes, Delaware has been good to us. We live in *Slower, Lower Delaware,* near the seaside towns of Lewes and Rehoboth Beach. Unlike many beach resorts, the arts and culture are celebrated here. Our retirement pursuits of painting for Paul and writing for me found a happy home.

And because we're always hungry we have tried the many restaurants with eclectic food choices—just footsteps from the ocean waves. If you travel to the East Coast, you really need to check out Delaware.

The CPAP Adventure

After years of hearing Paul snore, which didn't really bother me as I'm a sound sleeper, I felt I could no longer ignore the many times his breathing seemed to stop for a few seconds, followed by a big gasp. I was sure he had sleep apnea, and figured I needed to address it with his doctor and him, even though it was a bit late in the game. Around the same time, Paul was diagnosed with a mild heart arrhythmia. I asked his cardiologist if his sleep apnea had anything to do with his heart issue, and surprise, surprise—it did. So, after putting him on a low dose heart medication, off we trotted to the pulmonologist, a perky middle-aged woman who ran a few tests and broke the news to Paul. He now has a BiPAP machine, (similar to a CPAP so I'll just call it a CPAP, which is more familiar to most people).

He started to rebel against the idea, saying, "I'd rather die in my sleep"—to which the doctor responded with a smile, "You should be so lucky. You could end up with a stroke, and then what?" He met his match—this spunky lady who could tell it like it is with a cagey smile.

Aside from the first night when he threw his face mask across the room after I couldn't stop my nervous giggling, his adjustment has been a breeze. Though I do recall the time we were babysitting grandchildren in New Jersey. The kids were asleep, and since their parents went to an overnight wedding, they insisted we sleep in their bedroom. We crawled into bed after Paul put on his mask. I looked warily at their big dog, Bella.

"Don't worry. Annie promised she'll sleep in her dog bed next to the wall." My heart started to race when I saw Bella stand up and start to walk stealthily around to Paul's side of the bed.

"Bella—nooo!" I yelled in a loud whisper. Too late. She hopped onto the bed as Paul sat bolt upright, getting tangled in his air hose and spewing muffled profanities as poor Bella ran for her life.

Paul has started to tell me he can't get back to sleep after he wakes up to pee at 4 a.m. because apparently now *I* am snoring so loud.

"Well, that's easy to fix. Get ear plugs," I told him. I did feel kind of bad that besides being wired for sound with his CPAP machine, he has earplugs stuffed in his ears too, which by the way, he claims don't work.

I suggested he think of my snoring as rhythmic ocean waves, like the deafening noise machines our kids thought were indispensable to their babies and toddlers getting a good night sleep. Our grandkids are all going to need hearing aids by the time they're 30.

Anyway, I did try anti-histamines and steroid nose drops, thinking my problems might be allergies, but nothing worked. I am stalling on getting a sleep study to check for sleep apnea. Imagine both of us hooked up to machines. It will look like our very own Intensive Care Unit—so romantic.

I Will Never Be a Contestant on *Cupcake Wars*

###

I wonder if we have certain genes that decide whether we like to cook versus bake (as in cakes and cookies). It's not that I hate to bake, but depending on the recipe, there is so much exact measuring of important things like baking powder and baking soda and cream of tartar. Chemistry wasn't my strong suit. And say what you want—I think the batter always tastes better than the cake.

Plus, you can screw the whole thing up if you leave it in the oven 10 minutes too long. The gooey, chewy brownies are now hockey pucks, cemented to the pan.

Even though I could never be a contestant on *Cupcake Wars*, I always tried to use my imagination so I wouldn't traumatize our children with unadorned birthday cakes. Pressed into the frosting were tiny plastic football players, miniature ballerinas, and the Fisher-Price "little people"—all placed as if they were throwing a football, spinning in a pirouette, or sitting on the potty. Remember those cute Fisher-Price itty-bitty potties?

However, the "Happy Birthday" on top of the cake always looked like it was written by someone who just stumbled out of a bar. I could never quite get the hang of writing with a steady hand. Random curlicues around the edge were the extent of my decorative talent.

Maybe I don't love to bake because I don't have a sweet tooth. I crave salt and grease—although that does sound gross. I meant grease as in butter, hollandaise sauce, drippy bacon—all right, I guess I did mean grease. I have, over the years, tried to eat healthier. After all, as a retired nurse, I should know better. And I do like vegetables. I have the potential to be a vegetarian. Not a vegan, though—I love my cheese.

Cooking, as in making turkey tetrazzini with heavy cream, parmesan, and dry vermouth swirled in, is more my cup of tea—actually, change that to a glass of red wine while I'm cooking, along with some Josh Groban songs blasting in the background.

While I prefer cooking over baking, it doesn't mean I haven't had my share of culinary flops. And I'm a bit messy when I cook. My best creations result in grease splattering all the way into the living room—though that can happen even with a cheeseball.

One time in my younger days, I made an impressive salad for company with greens, red onion, baby shrimp and a citrus mayo dressing. When I dumped the thawed shrimp from the bag, I didn't seem to notice they weren't the pink color of cooked shrimp. My guests all had puzzled looks as they chewed on their sushi. I still can't believe no one got sick.

Our smoke alarms get good practice, so I feel very safe sleeping at night. Sometimes I have a good save, like, "The flavor of brussels sprouts is so much better when they're a little charred," which by the way, is true.

Oh, and the time I went to help out when our oldest daughter had her first baby. I pulled the chicken out of the oven in its glass baking dish and set it on the hot cook top of the stove to make gravy. The glass exploded all over the place, and our daughter, one day home from the hospital, came flying into the kitchen with a horrified look on her face. Her husband calmly swept up the broken glass, wondering what the rest of the week would bring.

I also tend to triple a good ingredient because how can you go wrong with too much turmeric? What's turmeric? It's the trendy new spice that might reduce inflammation, relieve the pain of arthritis, help with depression, etc. etc. The key word here is *might*. Anyway, the last time I made my award-winning chicken soup, I tripled the turmeric, and ended up with bitter, pungent tasting broth and chicken the color of a pumpkin. I don't want to give turmeric a bad name. A pinch goes a long way.

Just because I like to cook doesn't mean I like to spend all day in the kitchen, chopping and simmering. Note that I said *chop*, not mince, which means to chop into tiny pieces. I don't have that kind of patience. Why don't I get a food processor? Well, if you remember, I am a minimalist. A sharp knife plus a cutting board and I'm good.

One experience confirmed my feelings about a knife's utility. One of our daughters got a food processor as a gift and asked me to help her put it together. After we struggled through five pages of assembly directions, we ended up with what looked like a failed eighth grade science project, resembling a space shuttle with razor sharp blades jutting from the sides. I think it was returned. She's a minimalist like me.

Squeaky Floorboards

###

I have seen movies where the actress sneaks out in the middle of the night for an affair and slithers back into bed at 5 a.m., with her husband none the wiser. Paul is such a light sleeper that I could never get away with that, despite the fact that such a nefarious thing would never cross my mind.

I'm still doing research on when his deep REM sleep occurs. Why? Well, if he is not in that blessed state of sleep, he hears the floorboards squeak as I tiptoe into the kitchen and grab a handful of chips to quell the hunger that developed during my last hour of insomnia. Forget trying to get back into bed without a sound, as my shrinking torso needs to climb up on a stool and hop, backwards onto my much too high mattress.

I have *always* had a problem with squeaky floorboards. Whenever I'd attempt to go back to our bedroom 45 years ago, after rubbing the back of Brian, our 9-month-old baby who was teething, I'd have to do gymnastics getting from the room to the hallway. I would rub his back with a lighter and lighter stroke, then slip my hand away, take a few steps to the doorway, and with my arms hanging on the door frame, straddle my legs over the squeaky floorboards in the hallway.

Once I didn't move fast enough, and as I saw Brian start to get up on his knees, I dove under the crib. After a few minutes of quiet, I peeked out from under the crib and saw him standing next to the rail. When I dove back under again, my contact popped out onto the 1970's shag carpet, which I never found until the next day.

So, you probably think I had spoiled babies because I didn't let Brian fuss and cry. Well, I was desperate because we had other sleeping children who would just as soon start their day at 4 a.m., and I would scrub my kitchen with a toothbrush for an extra two hours of sleep.

Hashtags

Hashtags remain elusive little symbols that have managed to get the better of me. You know what I'm talking about, right? Well, in case you don't, they look like the lines on a Tic Tac Toe game, or the pound sign on a phone. Despite my research on Google, hashtags remain a mystery. From what I read, the # symbol is now being used on social media to help users find messages with a certain theme. I see posts with "#fine art," or "#adorable black cats," or "#surprised." I have tried to use them in my book marketing, to no avail. Either I'm not using them correctly, or their users belong to a secret club that I'm not allowed in.

Now, while I don't believe in the conspiracy theories that are going viral in our politics, I do have a conspiracy theory about ###. I think there is a Wizard of Oz type of creature hiding inside my computer who ignores my hashtags and me—age discrimination!

That's really all I have to say about them. And I am ok with some things forever being a puzzlement. When I get to heaven, I'll ask God to explain them to me, as well as all the other mysteries of life. Google will be glad for the break.

My Itchy Husband

###

"**Y**ou and Daddy were made for each other," I hear from our kids, and not always in a flattering way.

In some ways, though, Paul and I are very different. He cannot sit still. That is, unless he's watching football on TV or reading a book on the beach. No—he needs to be busy. Prior to the pandemic lockdown in Delaware, he had golf on Monday and Wednesday, art class on Friday, the gym in between, and summer days at the beach or the pool. When we used to have a sailboat, he jumped at the chance to drive three hours to the boat, whether it was just to check on it, or polish the teak with wax. And trust me, I am not complaining.

Because I, on the other hand, love my solitude and need my space. I have heard that from so many of my friends that I think it might be a female thing, though I don't mean to stereotype. I just need quiet time to think, and write, and meditate, and periodically unscramble my brain without too much sensory overload.

I remember a neighbor whose husband was always by her side. One day I saw him handing her clothes pins as she hung each piece of wet laundry on the clothes line back in the '70s. And no, I wasn't the least bit jealous.

We were driving home from our annual Florida winter trip one year. If you read my first book, you know that Paul does 90 percent of the driving and you know why.

Anyway, Paul had a miserable cold, though I don't have the slightest idea how you get a cold while relaxing in Florida. We got to the Hampton Inn in South Carolina and collapsed after nine hours in the car.

"Paul, since you feel like crap, why don't we spend an extra night in the hotel so you can rest?" I asked after dinner.

"Absolutely not. We're on the road by 8 a.m. tomorrow morning."

"Paul, listen to reason. I would consider it a gift to stay an extra day in bed, sleeping and watching TV if I had a bad cold, not to mention eating the bacon at their breakfast buffet."

"Well, I'm not you."

So off we went at 8 a.m. the next morning. I forgot that he had a crucial meeting with the US Treasury Department at the end of the day.

Please God—No Head Lice
or Cookie Exchanges

###

That used to be my prayer at Christmas, as right on schedule every winter, we got letters from the school—alerting us about the dreaded bug taking up residence in an unfortunate student's head of hair. One Christmas Eve we were in church and my friend leaned over to say her sister's kid was found to have head lice that morning. We both exchanged looks of horror. This bug had no respect for the holidays.

When the inevitable happened, I was in a tizzy for weeks. I left the medicated shampoo on our kids' scalps a tad longer than recommended, for good measure, unaware that back in the day, this was an older treatment that could be toxic if the directions weren't followed. Sorry, kids.

Anyway, the electric bill skyrocketed, as I vacuumed and washed sheets and blankets, and vacuumed again. I suffocated all the stuffed animals in plastic bags for weeks. And now my head is starting to itch—happens every time I talk about it.

My other holiday anxiety was the annoying "cookie exchange." I didn't like them then and I don't like them now. Why? Well, back in the '70s, I actually liked baking the traditional Christmas cookies—loaded with butter, nuts, and sprinkles. I even made my grandmother's kiffles, and was on my feet so long rolling out the dough, that my varicose veins progressed to the next level. I only made a few batches of each cookie—not the quantity my friends made that would last until February. Therefore, I wasn't looking forward to giving them away in a cookie exchange.

One year in church, a priest was addressing the stress of the holidays. He suggested we try doing only the activities that give us joy. Now that our children were older, was that permission to stop baking cookies? Paul didn't mind. He told me the powdered sugar covering my walnut butter balls always made him choke.

Now I could play Christmas music while I decorated, shopped, sent out cards, and bought supermarket cookies (without the guilt). Now, some of you know that I'm a terrible shopper. But I am on a mission in December, running around stores like a deer in headlights. So where is my joy in that? Well, it's all about the meaningful gift. Not expensive gifts—just meaningful.

I know you are thinking, "Don't you miss the scent of cinnamon and nutmeg during the holidays?" Well, you do know there are candles for that, right?

I hadn't been to a cookie exchange in ages, until I got an invitation in our retirement community a few years ago. The directions seemed complicated. Bake some to share the night of the exchange, and assemble bunches of cookies so everyone could go home with a sample packet of our creations. This meant I had to do math.

I also didn't realize that cookie exchanges now required a trip to Michael's for cutesy holiday containers with ribbons and sparkles. Instead, I piled my cookie samples onto squares of aluminum foil and crimped up the edges. Piling them all in a roasting pan, they looked more like 12 little Cornish hens just out of the oven. I was mortified when I placed them next to all my neighbors' colorful containers.

Thank God the cookie exchanges were a phase. Now it's just eat, drink, and be merry—sometimes exchanging silly gifts. And head lice are just a distant memory. That is, until I get a panicked call from our daughter on Christmas Eve.

Christmas 2019

We had our daughter's family here in Delaware one year for Christmas. Half are vegetarian, but I was calm about what to make for dinner on Christmas day. We would have our usual traditional prime rib roast and I would also make a meatless lasagna. Thank God they are not vegan anymore, so I could finally use fresh mozzarella.

The logistics of Christmas Eve still had to be worked out. They wanted to walk around the eclectic shopping area of Rehoboth Beach, 25 minutes from our home, during the afternoon. Since we planned to go to 4 o'clock Mass at St. Edmond's (down in Rehoboth Beach), I suggested they go ahead of us, and Paul and I would meet them later at the church.

Off they went, after I reminded them that because it was Christmas Eve, and the church only had street parking, they needed to get there early.

Paul and I left at 3 p.m. for St Edmond's—yep, an hour early. "Mary Ann, you better get on the phone and remind them to get there soon if they want a parking spot."

Oh geez, here we go with the parking panic. And it didn't look good, with the heavy traffic going down Rt.1 headed into Rehoboth. I called the granddaughter whose phone is always on alert. "Hi, honey. We're on our way. Where are you now?"

"Oh Grandma, we're in a salon getting our nails done."

"You're where? Are you almost done? Where's your Dad?"

"Yeah, we're almost finished. Daddy's out walking on Rehoboth Ave."

I looked over at Paul, who was muttering that he didn't see one parking spot. "Honey, let me hop out while you search. This way I can flag down the kids when I see them."

I walked across the street to the church, and realized the building was already full, and ushers were directing parishioners to the parish hall next door. People were pouring into the hall, which was on the lower level of the building. I called Paul's cell phone with the update; then I started down the steps to find the hall was filling quickly. I must have looked like I was about to cry, because the usher asked me, "How many?" After I said six, he pointed to the front of the hall on the side, under windows that looked out to the walkway.

I called our granddaughter and explained where to go. As they came through the door, I waved my arms like a crazy woman at the two young ladies and their mother with their painted nails—all accounted for except Eleanor's husband.

"He's looking for a parking spot," said El. We scanned the stragglers through the window, coming down the walk.

"There he is!" He was standing there, trying to figure out which building we were in. I started banging on the window, and after we found a way to open it, Paul and I both started screeching, "Craig!" Not only did we embarrass the two teenagers, but startled the congregation who were just settling into a reverent quiet. Craig made eye contact with us, and all was well.

Afterward, Craig, the Jerry Seinfeld of the family, said that when he looked down into the open windows, we looked like a bunch of desperate hostages pleading for him to free us.

Yep, it was the Christmas miracle—somehow, we all pulled it together.

Never Rush a Prime Rib

#

I mentioned in the last essay that I cooked a prime rib and lasagna on Christmas day. Please don't ask me how I accomplished this in the same oven, because I don't remember.

As we have prime rib only on Christmas, I need to check the Internet each year for cooking instructions, and we usually have good luck. If you follow the directions, it's hard to ruin this beast (as our vegetarian kids refer to it). Whether you want it cooked rare or medium well, it's all about the oven temperature.

One year we were traveling to the homes of our kids, and Paul suggested we have our own romantic pre-Christmas Eve, exchanging gifts, before we left. "And let's have a prime rib that night," said Paul. "We could be eating bamboo shoots when we get to the kids."

I went food shopping that morning and realized when I got home that I left the prime rib in a bag at the self-checkout. That should have been a sign that things were starting to unravel. I called the store and they said they found it and put it back in the case. So I drove back to find the prime rib that I bought, which was the perfect size for two people—gone. I chose another that was really too big and went to customer service to show them my receipt and pay the difference.

He said, "You don't owe us anything. Merry Christmas!"

The rest of the day I finished wrapping presents and started to pack our suitcases, when I looked at the clock. Oh, geez! When was I supposed to put the rib roast into the oven? It'll be 8 o'clock before it's done.

After pre-heating the oven to 500 degrees (per the Internet), I took the roast from the refrigerator and popped it in.

Mistake #1: I was supposed to let it get to room temperature before sticking it in the oven. After 15 minutes of cooking, I turned the oven temp down to 325 degrees, as directed (per the Internet).

"What time do you think we'll eat, honey?" asked Paul.

"If we're lucky—7:30. I screwed up the timing, so just have another glass of wine and watch the news." I got the rest of the dinner ready, and set the table, taking peeks periodically at the meat thermometer.

Then I heard, "If you keep opening the oven, Mary Ann, we'll be eating at midnight." And then, after another 15 minutes, "Smells good to me, Mary Ann. You don't want to over-cook a prize piece of meat like a prime rib."

"I think I know that, dear."

What a stupid idea—trying to cook something like this the night before a big trip.

At 7:45 I turned the temperature back up to 400 degrees (a no-no), and was on my hands and knees looking through the window, begging for it to be done.

8:30—the meat thermometer registered medium rare and we finally ate. No time for the roast to "rest." Even though it was nice and pink, it was like chewing shoe leather. Never rush a prime rib.

The Coronavirus

###

I cannot continue to write without acknowledging the elephant in the room—the pandemic. We were in our Florida rental February of 2020 when the coronavirus became the great disruptor of the world as we knew it. As this mysterious virus crept closer to our sphere, we became hypervigilant.

With the exception of the AIDS epidemic (that jolted the field of medicine), we had a comfort level whenever we spiked a fever because of historical figures like Louis Pasteur and Jonas Salk—along with the discovery of antibiotics, antivirals, and vaccines. We were invincible to the pompous little microbes of days gone by.

The pandemic has spread its ugly tentacles, taking far too many lives. And there is no one without some angst, for everyone has been touched in some way by COVID-19.

Because of the surrounding sadness and uncertainty, I think we keep searching, subconsciously, for any coping mechanism we can find. And like new life in the spring, which pokes its head through the cracks in the concrete, humor stubbornly makes its way to our psyches in tragedy. So—I keep writing.

Please know that I mean no disrespect. Hopefully, through my writing, I give others permission to smile.

In the very early days of the virus, saying to friends that we were "social distancing" sounded a little hoity-toity (sorry Paul Hoyt). But it didn't take long for most people to get on board. No hugging, or shaking hands, or getting closer than six feet—all this scary stuff happening way too fast.

On one of the last Sundays before our church in Florida stopped in-person services, we went to Mass. Paul's allergy had been a problem for weeks, and after he blew his nose in a tissue, I whipped out the Purell and gave it to him, so fellow parishioners wouldn't faint.

After we got back from Communion, I noticed a tissue on the floor in front of us. Oh geez—is that from us, or somebody else? I kicked it to the side, hoping Paul wouldn't see it. We sat down in the pew, and I could see Paul's eyes staring at the tissue. I knew exactly what he was thinking. If I pick that thing up, she's going to freak out. Out of the corner of my eye, I could see him reach into his pocket, counting his tissues. And then—I saw him kick the one on the floor further under the pew.

After we got outside, I said, "We should have picked that tissue up."

"I didn't because I know you too well!"

"Oh great, I know we don't have the virus, but what if we do and the poor janitor gets sick and starts the spread?"

"I guess you'll be the new *Typhoid Mary*."

And then came the decision. Do we go home early or stay and wait it out in sunny Florida? Paul was fine with staying in the sun. I, on the other hand, wanted the comfort of home, closer to our kids, even though we couldn't visit them. We compromised and bumped up our departure date.

It was not a restful drive home. We threw our belongings in the car with handfuls of Clorox wipes that I scrounged from the rental. A neighbor gave Paul doggy poop bags to wear when he pumped gas. The long, green, plastic covers on his arms made him look like he was about to operate on the gas pump.

The Hampton Inn in South Carolina was the halfway point in our trip. No one was wearing a mask at this point in the pandemic. Three other people decided to crowd into the elevator with us, dragging their baggage. I started to get woozy from holding my breath until we reached the third floor.

"I need to wipe down the hard surfaces before you put your wallet and stuff down," I said to Paul before he unloaded his pockets onto the dresser, almost forgetting the biggest culprits—the remote and the door knobs.

From my student days in the operating room, my brain went into microbe mode. Paul told me I was starting to drive him nuts.

Eating with plastic forks, the frozen dinners I had packed in the cooler and cooked in the hotel's microwave were a culinary treat. "It's still cool in the middle," Paul informed me. This is the same guy who would prefer that all his food was warm at home. Not piping hot—just warm.

"Let me put it in the microwave a couple more minutes."

"Well, if we can't get it hot, I'll run out and get us take-out somewhere," said the man who doesn't like his food piping hot.

"Oh no you won't—I put too much energy into this camping trip!"

After two nine-hour days on the road, we made it home. Now we could social distance in our own little cocoon. Back in reality, and sheltering in place, we learned the extent of the pandemic, with sobering daily briefings from the task force. To be continued…

My Succulent Sausages

Retired, here in Delaware, I am the grandmother who now sits in a beach chair handing out snacks and praising the grandkids for every crashing wave they ride or sandcastle they build. When they were tiny, I'd hold their little wet bodies on my lap; and welcome sand pedicures with my feet in a hole, followed with a bucket of salt water dumped on top (my feet—not me).

However, I secretly wished I could be the grandmother who rides a boogie board and dives under a giant breaker. One of the grandkids said recently that she can't wait to visit us and eat one of Grandma's *succulent* sausages for breakfast. Now that's the kind of affirmation I need. For other desperate grandmothers out there who are trying to redefine their beach identity—they were Banquet maple-flavored breakfast sausages. Look in the frozen aisle.

One year I came a hair closer to being the *cool* grandma. Every summer visit to Delaware includes a trip to Funland, a family owned amusement park with rides that I would call relatively tame except for the upside down one.

On each visit, I carefully looked at the expressions of the adults coming off the Sea Dragon. Most were laughing and holding the hands of little six year olds. And then I checked out the trajectory of the ride—forward and backward in a rhythmic motion, not terribly fast, no jerky moves or flipping upside down. So I finally gathered my nerve and offered to go on this ride with one of the younger ones.

"Sit near the center of the Sea Dragon, Grandma. It's not as scary as the ends." What a sweet child, thinking of my welfare. The ride began. Not so bad. Oh—wait. Nobody told me that when our side went up in the air, I'd be looking at the ground. I threw my hands in front of the glasses dangling off my nose. Then, like an eagle, we swooped back down. And then we went back up. I started to feel dizzy. I was afraid my nausea would progress to something else if I screamed.

When will it stop? Will I be the historic first to have projectile vomiting which won't be pleasant for those on the ground? They'll have to turn kids away for the rest of the afternoon while they clean up the Sea Dragon. How mortifying. My crazy thoughts helped to pass the eternal time it took to stop the torture.

I staggered off the ride, feeling my equilibrium completely out of whack. My daughter looked at my pale, expressionless face, debating whether to call 911.

"I'm ok," I whispered. "I just need to sit." And for the next hour, I sipped a bottle of ice cold water, pressing the bottle to my forehead. I wondered if the grandkids were saying, "What was she thinking? She can't even ride a wave."

Yep, there's a part of me that's a wimp, but that's okay. Hopefully that doesn't define me. I'm very content with being known for my succulent sausages.

Babysitting the Pets

###

I never had a pet growing up. Therefore, I was always a bit squeamish around animals. I was probably traumatized by the childhood experience I had with a dog. I was 7 years old, walking by myself to school one day (yes, we could do that back then). Out of nowhere, a large black dog came bounding towards me (and yes, back then dogs could roam without a leash). I froze in my tracks as it yanked off my mitten with its teeth and ran away. Trembling, I walked the rest of the way in tears.

Now, from what I know today, since the tail was wagging, it's quite possible that it just wanted to play catch with my mitten. I guess I'll never know what Cujo's intent was. But it doesn't matter. The psychological damage was done.

I needed a crash course in dogs, because babysitting the grandkids meant I couldn't hide under my bed from their canines. I learned fast that the dogs would be easier than the kids.

I had a few unsettling experiences while babysitting, however. I found Bella in my bedroom one day next to my purse that I left open on the floor. The carpet was damp around the purse, as were open gum wrappers. Oh no! I knew there were some forbidden foods that dogs were never to ingest under risk of death. I immediately googled the ingredients of sugarless gum, to find that xylitol was a dog killer. Breaking out in a sweat, I unraveled the wet scraps of wrapping to find that we were in the clear. No xylitol.

Then there was the night I babysat our 3-month-old grandson, who was asleep in his crib. Around midnight, I heard a gasping, choking-like cough. Oh God—the baby! I ran upstairs, banged open the door and hovered over the sleeping little cherub. To be sure he was okay, I placed my ears to his mouth to listen for breathing and placed my trembling hand on his chest to feel the rhythmic rise and fall. Hmmm…

I tip-toed out of his room to check the other living creature in the house—Mugsy, the big black English bulldog, who was asleep in the master bedroom. I put on the overhead light and thought—"Oh my God, it was the dog!" His breathing was shallow, and when I yelled his name, he didn't stir. The same way we were taught to do CPR, yelling, "Annie, Annie are you okay?" while shaking the mannequin, I yelled, "Mugsy, Mugsy, wake up!" while grabbing him by the shoulders.

In desperation, I went for the cheese (no, not the defibrillator). I ran down the stairs, grabbed a piece of American cheese from the refrigerator, ran back up the stairs and waved it in front of his nose. He opened one eye, gulped down the cheese, and went back to sleep.

"Sorry Mom," said our daughter when she got back. "I forgot to tell you that Mugsy does that sometimes. I think he has allergies."

Mugsy tested my sanity one other time. I put the same child, now 3 years old and newly potty-trained, to bed for a nap after I clapped and cheered for the present he left me in the potty. I came out of the bedroom two minutes later to empty the potty into the toilet and found it empty. Was I losing my mind? I was sure I didn't empty it, and got down on my hands and knees to stare into the potty, as if I would find a clue. Now, don't roll your eyes. I found one—three black strands of hair (or should I say fur). If Mugsy wasn't shedding, I wouldn't have been able to solve the case.

I then went into panic mode again. I called the vet, whose number I found on a refrigerator magnet, and explained what happened to the receptionist. There was a long pause. "Oh my—I'll check with the vet. I know that dogs eat other dogs' poop, but (pause again), let me check." What seemed like an hour later, she came back to the phone telling me to check him every hour for signs of lethargy or vomiting. "Sweet Jesus, how do these things happen to me?"

Mugsy was fine. I told Annie what happened after she came home from work. Alarmed, she asked worriedly, "He did what??? Is he okay?"

"He is but I'm not. May I uncork the bottle of Cabernet I saw on the counter?"

I think Paul needs to take a few turns at babysitting the pets. They'll stay out of harm's way when he's in charge. After all, he saved Ebbitt, the pet yellow lab of our Texas grandchildren, from sniffing a tarantula. You don't want to know the details. A broom was involved.

Rehearsing My Lines

On my way to the doctor I find myself talking to myself in the car, rehearsing what I am going to say. As a retired RN, I want them to know they are speaking to a fellow professional, so I don't want to come across as a scatter-brained hypochondriac. I need to think like a nurse and state the main problem, with pertinent details to clarify. It was painful to accompany my mother to the doctor. The history she gave was filled with descriptive details that could fill the whole page of a book, if I didn't butt in to try and summarize. I didn't do that very much though, as I would get the evil eye and she would raise her hand to me, saying, "Stop!"

Paul also has issues with me butting in, but sometimes I have no choice. I watch the doctor's eyes get wider and wider as he tells him about the golf game five days ago when he first felt a pain in his back on the 17th tee, but then it felt a little better, that is, until he got on the elliptical two days ago at the gym, so he decided not to cut the grass today and take some ibuprofen, which hasn't relieved the pain.

So, to get to the point on *my* sick visits to the doctor, I practice my spiel in the car. I find I do the same with the dentist, and the ophthalmologist...

Hopefully, at the eye doctor, I get my questions in before they start with the lenses. "Is number one better, or number two? Number one, or two, or how about three." I hate that part. So I chime back, "Can you go back to number one, and can you go a little slower? Four hundred dollars is going into number one or two."

As long as we are talking about all things medical, do any of you ladies get bladder infections? I like to call them UTIs—sounds more acceptable for casual conversation. Well, as we get older we are more prone to them. One of the best ways to prevent them is to drink a lot of water, which I do now, but I didn't do then. The biggest motivation for upping my daily water consumption?—I am *done* giving urine specimens.

Why? Well, you need to drink a bottle of water on the way to the doctor's office, to make sure your bladder is full enough to pee. By the time you get there, you wish you were wearing a Depends. And then—do you know how hard it is to pee into a sterile cup the size of a shot glass? My plan is working. I'm on 18 months and counting of bladder health.

In fact, Paul and I are relatively healthy, despite all the doctors' appointments scribbled on our calendar and the content of our discussions at cocktail parties.

The need to share hasn't changed. In 1975, we shared detailed accounts of our babies' births over a glass of wine—the worst labor and delivery of all time, the drama of an emergency C-section, and the drive-through birth. We all knew someone who had a baby in her arms two hours after the first twinge in her belly—her hair and make-up still intact. So unfair.

Now, we talk about colonoscopies.

TV Channels for Peaceful Waiting Rooms

#

On my last visit to the ophthalmologist, pre-pandemic, the parking lot looked like Walmart during the holidays, (or should I say Walmart—all year long). I figured they must be giving out eyeballs. At 10 a.m. the average age in the waiting room looked to be about 80, with all the younger clients either at work or school.

By the way, because of the political climate, no more Fox News or CNN on the TVs in doctors' waiting rooms anymore. They can't risk somebody losing a tooth because of a walker heaved in their direction.

No, it's all HGTV. With all the time I have spent in waiting rooms, I could remodel a fixer-upper and flip it, becoming a wealthy woman in retirement.

There is one show that does a renovation for a lucky couple who have to stay out of their house for a week. When the excited couple walks blindfolded back into their home to view the miraculous change, the designer takes off the blindfolds with a flourish. It cracks me up that I have never heard, "Aagh—I hate it. What was I thinking—letting you remove our paisley wall paper and rip up our nasty carpet. I want my dated furniture back!" No, it's all gushing praise. Although, I bet there is at least one fail, but we probably won't see the tape!

Have you noticed there is no way to switch the channel unless you climb on a chair? I'm getting tired of home renovation ideas. I think the next time I go, I'll ask them to turn on the Food Network.

Buying a Mattress

###

Most of you know how decision challenged I am, especially when shopping. For example, Santa Claus used to bring each of our three daughters a doll every Christmas. I know—horrifying. But this was back in the '70s. Customers came and went in the doll aisle of Toys R Us, as I hovered—scrutinizing every plastic bundle of joy. All three had to be able to cry, burp, and pee. When I put a chubby-cheeked redhead on my shoulder and tried to burp it, the security camera police put me on their watch list.

But I really met my Waterloo a few months ago when we decided to buy a new mattress. "We definitely need a firmer one, but one that's squishy enough on top to be comfortable," I said to Paul.

"Ok, whatever that means."

Nobody warned me of the modern, state of the art mattresses called *hybrids*. Skeptically, I listened to the sales pitch—"Luxurious foam on top of individually wrapped coils. And you need to lie on them for at least 10 minutes to get the feel."

Well, that was awkward—having a salesman hover, while we tossed and turned on the beds. "Any chance you have some paperwork you could do while we figure this out?" I asked. He obliged us and went to his desk in the corner to look over invoices while listening to the Giants-Steelers game, all the while peering over his glasses at the two of us trying our favorite sleep positions on multiple mattresses.

We made our choice—and, no pressure. The store policy stated we were allowed two exchanges within 120 days.

"Is it my imagination, or am I sagging in this thing?" I asked Paul the first night.

"No, you're not exaggerating. And, I feel like I'm sliding off the edge every time I roll over." So we snuggled a bit closer, and decided to return it. I went on Google and found charts that rate mattresses on how supportive they are for bad backs, bad hips, and—oh my—good sex.

Back at the store, I explained the mattress was too soft. After tossing and turning on a few more, and getting thoroughly confused, we had a firmer model delivered. Paul was asleep in seconds. I, on the other hand, flailed around in the bed, trying to get comfortable. Why didn't I remember this mattress feeling like our granite counter top in the store? I felt like Goldilocks, sleeping in Papa bear's bed. Maybe I just needed to break it in, like a new pair of sneakers.

I did venture into the store a third time, saying to myself, "The third time's a charm." Staring at 25 mattresses, I almost broke out into hives at the thought of making another switch. Five minutes later, I bolted out of the store.

Even though we had another 115 days to change our minds, there was no way I was going to step foot in that store again. Unlike Goldilocks, I was done trying to find the mattress that was *just right*.

Are you thinking I should get one of those foam toppers? Out of the question. If the bed gets any higher, I'll need a ladder to get up onto the mattress. As it is, I use a stepstool, and am contemplating putting a trampoline next to the bed in case I fall out.

We are keeping this very expensive, very firm mattress—'til death do us part.

Tripping (and not on drugs)

I think I might be getting that football encephalopathy I've been hearing about on the news. No, I never played football. It's just that my klutzy body trips frequently, with an occasional face plant. The granddaughters I traumatized years ago with an unfortunate fall leaving the library, now just roll their eyes and say matter-of-factly to any bystanders, "Don't worry. Our grandma just tripped again. She does that a lot."

Part of the reason is, I don't pay attention when I walk fast. Once in the grocery store, I realized that I ran right past the butter almond ice cream in the freezer section; so I attempted to make a U-turn with the top half of my body and my right foot, leaving my left foot still rooted to the ground. What's wrong—you can't visualize that?

I am really not that old, unless you consider 70 old. However, I feel old every time Paul gently grabs my elbow and says, "Watch it," 50 times an hour when we're out walking on uneven sidewalks. I know he does it out of love, though I also think he doesn't want to be suspected of spousal abuse. I still have a mark on my face (six years later) from tripping over our ironing board while coming back from the bathroom in the middle of the night. I smacked my face on our bedside table and needed to spend $75 on cover-up make-up so I could show up at our daughter's wedding.

Once I even tripped going up the steps of a tour bus, falling into the man in front of me who walked with a cane because of an old spinal injury. Poor guy—I'm sure that set him back.

A few clues to my tripping came when I recently went to physical therapy for treatment of arthritis in my neck. This was my first ever physical therapy appointment and I didn't know what to expect. I got a very nice therapist that did an assessment. He had me do some head and torso turns, all the while observing me critically. "Yes, you do have significant muscle tension in your neck." Well, yes, I know that, but I smiled sweetly as he went on.

"Do you know one hip is higher than the other? And one shoulder is not level?" He then asked me to look straight at his nose. I said, "I am."

"No you're not. Your head is tilting to the right." I started breaking out in a sweat.

"Okay—I came in here with a neck problem. Now I feel like a hot mess."

On the positive side—at least now I had a reason, or maybe more than one for my propensity to trip. And the hot packs and massage to my neck were worth this depressing knowledge.

I wasn't crazy about the neck exercises, though. I had to look straight ahead and tuck my chin to my chest (which gave me an instant double chin), and do this 10 times. I was going to ask him if I could go behind the curtain, but I thought it would be inconsiderate to make the accident victim with the bad back wait his turn.

I did notice a camaraderie with all the clients—you could feel the energy. I started to really get into my neck exercises. Watch a You Tube video of Bert, from Sesame Street, singing and acting out, "Doin' the Pigeon." That was me, from the shoulders up.

My Memory

If you speak to my children, please vouch for my cognitive ability. Now, I'm telling you this in confidence. My memory is shot. Plus, sometimes I get the generations mixed up. But who wouldn't? We have four children and ten grandchildren and, as I said in the previous chapter, I've had a few face plants on the ground.

More importantly—I read somewhere that our memories adapt to a constant influx in today's information overload world. As long as I can remember the year and the name of the president, I'm safe. That's what they always ask you in the hospital.

I was visiting one of our daughters a few months ago and she asked me, "Mom, do you feel like you are forgetting things a lot?" She caught me off guard, and I responded calmly, "Well, maybe a little. I've just got a lot on my mind."

The next day she asked, "Did I upset you yesterday when I asked you about your memory?"

"No, of course not," I lied. I will look at this conversation as a gift—a *heads up*, if you will, to the future. I can now monitor my speech so they don't stick me in a Memory Care Unit before it's time.

That weekend, we were on our way to see our New England kids, and I found out that they, too, were in on the conference about mom. Damn!

After we got back home, I got a call from our youngest, the nurse. "Mom, we decided you're ok. We think you have selective memory. And you are just your normal ditzy self."

"Well, thank you for the evaluation, my dear. And, by the way, now I don't trust any of you!"

Just because I remember the year, the name of the president, and the names of all the perennials in my garden doesn't mean that I don't need a list for everything else. I have perfected my traveling bag inventory of things to remember when going on road trips; because, if I don't put shoes on my list, I'll be wearing my sneakers the whole time.

As we've gotten older, some things have more importance, like our medicine. And my make-up is right up there with Paul's CPAP machine.

Then come the cell phone chargers and—never forget underwear. I mean—I know we can replace some of this stuff in Walmart, but with my perfected list, I've got it covered.

I have another, more extensive list for when we go to our beach rentals, which includes all of our beach paraphernalia and our own bathmat. What's wrong—you think that's odd? I have a friend who asked if she could have a copy of my list. What affirmation—someone else likes to place her newly showered toes on a snowy white bathmat from home that was washed in bleach! Let me know if you'd like a copy too.

Now, lastly, and this may seem obvious—don't forget to put your suitcase in the car. A few years ago, we were on the road to see family, when our neighbor called my cell phone to ask why a suitcase was sitting in our driveway for five hours. I won't tell you who it belonged to, but someone had to buy his underwear at Walmart.

Walking Through My Neighborhood

I am a solitary walker. It's when I do my thinking, meditating, and daydreaming. I know—not much mindfulness going on when my thoughts need to be captured by a lasso most of the time. I am also not a daily walker, although that is my goal. And since I prefer the fresh air and sunshine to a sweaty gym, I am looking for strategies to deal with the wind and rain.

In the grocery store, I can do 10,000 steps backtracking the aisles multiple times for things I forgot, or searching for my lost grocery cart that I left in aisle 3 (or maybe it was 12) when I ran to aisle 8 for bread. Add another 2,000 steps if I lose my cart the day before Thanksgiving in the crowd of shoppers. That's when paranoia sets in, as I start looking at the size of the turkeys in everybody else's cart. I mean, it is possible they took my cart by mistake.

But back to my solitary walking—I need to change my route. We have a group of gentlemen who bike every morning through the neighborhood. I seem to meet them multiple times head on, as they bike in and out of the cul-de-sacs.

Me—first pass: "Good morning." Response—times six bikers: "Good morning."

Me—second pass: "Mornin'—again." Response—times six: "Mornin'—again."

Me—third pass: "Hope you make it in before the rain." Response—times six: "Hope so!"

Me—fourth pass: I pretend I am on my cell phone.

Pedicures

#

I want to tell you how I've evolved regarding my perception of pedicures. If you read my first book, I mentioned that I mostly did my own, as I preferred a hair appointment with a glorious head massage thrown in, rather than someone scrubbing the callouses on my feet. I'm sure you all thought I was nuts. I was, but I've come to my senses, partly because now my back hurts for days after attending to my toes. What was I thinking—not to appreciate that soothing warm water swirling around my feet and the pulsation of the neck massager in the chair.

The salons offering pedicures now hand you a menu of their services as big as the Applebee's food menu. With all the children starving in the world, I can't get myself to ask for the super deluxe pedicure, the salon's equivalent to a filet mignon. Do my calves really need a hot stone massage? Of course, I don't know what kind of salary these pedicurists get, so I suppose I could look at it from a different angle and give them a nice big tip—maybe for my next birthday.

One time at the nail salon, they were behind schedule and my feet were soaking longer than the normal allotted time as the nail technician finished with another client. Little did they know it felt like I got a bonus. The owner was so apologetic and told the tech to add the sugar scrub to my calves. Sugar never disappoints, however it's used. And to think I did nothing to deserve this extra pampering.

These hard-working nail techs are really special. I wonder if these ladies who turn everyone's tootsies with their yucky looking toes into Cinderella feet (or so we think) realize how they make our day.

Age is Relative

I am convinced that age is relative. If it wasn't for my recent cataract surgery, and the fact that I move around like Old Mother Hubbard when I first crawl out of bed in the morning, I would still think I'm 30. And that's because my brain hasn't caught up with my body.

I love hanging out on the phone as if I were a teenager, and dancing to my Spotify playlist while I am Swiffering. If Simon & Garfunkel come on the radio while I'm driving, there are no sounds of silence in my car.

And—I continue to make stupid mistakes. How can that be? Isn't there a cut-off date when everything starts to click? You all know the saying, "Please be patient. God isn't finished with me yet." Well, apparently, I've been a challenge.

Music, smells, images—they can all transport my brain to another era. We were at a party once, where the band was playing "Help, Help Me Rhonda," as Paul and I got out onto the dance floor. There is nothing like a sixties song to blur my reality. I shimmied my hips with what I thought was a foxy grin on my face, losing all track of time. I happened to be facing the band, and near the end of the song when I did an about face—reality struck. I saw a lot of other animated 65-year-old bodies, arms flailing and derrieres too wide to be shimmying in public—also with foxy grins on their faces. But as I said, age is relative. And the best part—unlike teenagers, with their budding self-esteem—we don't give a damn.

The Day My Cell Phone Took a Dive into the Toilet

###

Somebody with OCD does not consider a cell phone falling into the toilet a trivial thing. And it doesn't matter that it was "clean" water. I was lucky to find Clorox wipes in our daughter's bathroom, to sanitize the phone. Somehow, it came back to life. I can't remember if it was the hair dryer that resuscitated it or letting it sit in a bag of rice. Anyway, about six months later, it was acting up and I brought it to a shop that sold and repaired cell phones. He took the back off, peered into the guts of the phone and said, "It's obviously had water damage. In fact, I still see some moisture."

I had been carrying a phone in my pocket for six months with drops of toilet water? Did I need to advise this guy that he may need to use Purell when he was done?

Cell phone mishaps aside, I was just thinking how dependent we are on them. And how we take the instant gratification of talking to a friend for granted. Back in the '50s, my parents would gather us into the living room around the black, rotary dial phone to make the weekly call to our out-of-state grandparents. Long distance phone calls were made after 6 p.m. when the rates went down. "How have you been?" was followed (every single time) by, "How is your weather up there?"

My three siblings and I would line up single file to talk. I'd say, "Hi Grandma and Grandpa. How are you?" Then I was quickly moved aside for kid number two, as the clock was ticking. If I had anything else to say, I sat at the kitchen table and wrote a letter.

The Rhode Island beach cottage that we vacationed at with our kids didn't even have a phone in the '70s. I made calls from a pay phone in the evening, getting bitten up by the mosquitos swarming under a street light.

Yes, communicating is so much easier now. I just have to remember to hang onto my phone when I'm in the bathroom.

The Recliner

I was allowed to stay with my mother for a couple overnights in her assisted living facility following her short stay in the hospital. I slept in her motorized recliner, which I have to say was quite comfortable, once I figured out how to use it. It really wasn't hard—just a matter of pushing a button to raise the legs and recline. To get it back to the upright position, you pressed a different button.

The first morning I programmed my brain to wake up at 6:30. My mother moved as slow as most 90-plus-year-olds move, and as she was very independent, didn't want a lot of help. So, we had plenty of time to get out to the dining room by 8 a.m.

On the second day, my eyes popped open at 7:30. Holy crap—I slept in! Now, do you remember Kramer (from Seinfeld)? Well, imagine the next part with him in the recliner to get the visuals. I forgot this thing I slept in was motorized. Forgetting to push the button to get the chair into its upright position, I jumped up and landed on my hands and knees on the floor, with the recliner on top of me—my water that was in the attached cup holder all over me and the carpet. I somehow managed to pop back up, righting the lightweight recliner. I was more worried about giving my mother a heart attack than the condition of my limbs, but because she was hard of hearing, she slept through the whole thing.

By the way, they kept our breakfast warm, although the wait staff glanced at my bedraggled look, a bit puzzled.

The Frying Pan

###

Would you like to know a little about my mother? If you read my first book, you already know she was a prolific seamstress, making all our clothes with the exception of our underwear. She was also a nurse (like me), and had four children (like me). She was a friendly, outgoing person, but also very private. She didn't spill her guts to the world (like me).

On school mornings, my mother's scrambled eggs sat in the frying pan waiting for my three siblings and I to stumble down the steps of our Archie Bunker style house on a school morning.

A little side bar—my mother's eggs were good, but nothing could surpass the scrambled eggs my Grandfather McHugh made. One year, we spent a week in Scranton, PA with my maternal grandparents so my father could paint the house, uninterrupted, during the strike at the Bethlehem Steel. We'd come home, bragging about my grandfather's fluffy scrambled eggs, because he added a little bit of milk and stirred them slowly over a low heat. After the 20th fluffy eggs comment (and never mentioning my father's beautiful paint job), I could hear my dad mutter under his breath, with a bit of envy and hurt in his voice, "Scrambled eggs are scrambled eggs."

Most of our food was fried back then, in the large aluminum frying pan, like the haddock my mother bought from the fish truck that rang its bell in our neighborhood every Friday afternoon. Midday on Sundays, chicken spattered away in the frying pan on top of the stove, while a lemon meringue pie baked in the oven.

My stand-out memory of the frying pan is the night my father died, after living with cancer for five years. It was 1983, and my mother, my sister, and I drove home from the hospital, exhausted at 3 a.m. Once inside the house, my mother jumped into her mommy mode, despite losing her husband an hour before. Out came the frying pan. "I'm making you scrambled eggs and toast. You need to eat before you go to sleep. We have a big day ahead." Yep, that was our mother.

She was a woman of faith. Years later, as her health deteriorated, she spent her final months in a memory care unit. I used to pray, "When it is time, dear Lord, please take her gently."

One day, not long after, even though my breakfast would normally consist of coffee and whole grain toast, for some unknown reason, I got out the frying pan and made myself a scrambled egg. An hour later I got a call from my sister that our 94-year-old mother died peacefully in her sleep.

My Father

I need to give equal time to my father, as I have a lot of his traits. He was tall and lanky as a young man, and had light brown hair that turned a wavy, jet black as he got older.

As an adolescent, he cut hair in a barber shop on Saturdays, handing his salary of $.75 to his parents at the end of the day. After a stint in the Navy, he worked at the Bethlehem Steel Company, though in today's era, I know he would have been a successful graphic artist or cartoonist. His sketch of Popeye is now framed in the bedroom of a great grandchild. He did all the freehand art work on the 55 Campbell's soup can costumes worn by my brother's class in the Halloween parade in 1956. We should have gotten a lifetime supply of chicken noodle soup for the free marketing.

To say he was proud of his children would be an understatement. He told all his friends down at the Bethlehem Steel Company that I could spell "Carthaginian"—in the third grade. Of course, today they could probably spell that in pre-school. It's funny how tiny fragments of memory remain so clear in my mind. By the way, I just looked that word up, as I was never sure of its meaning. Hmm—why were we studying ancient history in third grade?

A great story-teller, my father had us sitting wide-eyed as he relayed the horrors of surviving Navy boot-camp—while my mother gave him the evil-eye because she was afraid he was scaring us. We couldn't get enough of the stories about recruits dropping like flies in the 90-degree heat during their running drills. And how proud we were to find out that, though he never stepped foot on a boat prior to serving in the Navy, he was one of the few sailors who never got seasick on the Navy ship.

His favorite story was how he stood at attention to honor the body of President Franklin D Roosevelt during the funeral procession along the streets of Washington, DC.

My Dad was intelligent and informed, despite the fact that he did not go to college. Because of his influence, I love to play Scrabble and I love talking about politics and the news.

We stopped at his grave with our kids in 1983, a few months after he died. Our son Brian, who was 8 years old at the time, plopped down suddenly on all fours and started to do a Michael Jackson break dance on the gravesite to show Grandpa. It wasn't hard to imagine my Dad laughing and proudly pointing out his grandson to all his new buddies in heaven.

Mount Everest

###

When we visit our children and their families, my body and its aging muscles have to get used to the layout of their homes, specifically the stairs. The *rise*, which is the height of each step, is a bit higher in a few of the houses—just enough to make it feel like I am climbing Mount Everest every time I venture to the second floor. Forget about carrying a basket of laundry up. I dread the day the railing pops off because of my breathless tugging. It won't be a pretty sight, with Grandma rolling down two flights of stairs.

Also, what's this business of arranging the beds against a bedroom wall? Paul and I slept in one of these rooms with a bed next to a wall. Since Paul needed a bedside table for his CPAP, he was on the outside; and because he was asleep first, I climbed in from the bottom. There was a window at mattress level, but I managed to squirm up to the top of the bed without rolling the wrong way and crashing through the screen. Getting under the covers was another Houdini feat—could have been a scene from *I Love Lucy*.

Before we went home, I insisted on washing the sheets and remaking the bed for Annie. I climbed up on the mattress, as there is no other way when the bed's against the wall. I yanked the fitted sheet up and tried to tuck it over the mattress corner, without losing my balance and flying out the window.

I had an emergency plan, just in case. I'd hang onto the windowsill until someone drove by. Hopefully, by then, my body wouldn't be sprawled over the front porch roof. I can just imagine our grandkids riding their bikes home, looking up, and yelling, "Grandma, you shouldn't be up there. It's not safe."

Regarding life and limb, I'm now more selective with what I do for my kids—and that would be folding laundry on the first floor.

The Scale

Ok, I will be honest. I am having trouble losing the last 10 pounds that would make me feel healthy. I didn't say svelte—I'm realistic. I have gone up a size (two sizes if you count my wedding gown).

However, the new me is downing all kinds of chia seeds and spicy vegetables (still not big on tofu)—and, I am determined to keep walking. Now that my plantar fasciitis is healed, the Christmas decorations are put away, the wind chill has died down, and my orthopedic doctor said my hips are not as bad as they feel—oh no, are you rolling your eyes again?

I am thrilled that I can now wear skinny jeans, and not because I'm skinny. You see, the fashion designers have gotten older themselves. They, too, want to wear skinny jeans, and realized they'll make a lot more money with blousy tops and sweaters that cover your butt. Such an optical illusion when I now look into a full-length mirror! Add the tiny sizes when I buy at Chico's—wow, I'm 29 again!

Speaking of tiny sizes, I had a scare one summer's day when visiting our grandchildren. It turned chilly and I wanted to switch from my shorts to jeans. I went up to use our granddaughter's bedroom to change and proceeded to pull on my size 10 jeans. I freaked out that I couldn't get my jeans over my knees. I looked at the size again, not understanding how that extra plate of lasagna the night before could have had such an immediate impact. And then I saw *my* size 10 jeans that I threw on the bed. I was shoving my leg into our granddaughter's "girls" size 10.

A big motivation to healthy eating is to stare at your shadow on the sidewalk when you're out walking—the image that walks in front of you when the sun is behind you in the sky. It's never flattering and, try as I might, my eyes keep fixating on the shapeless silhouette of the stranger in front of me that refuses to turn left down the next street.

I have discovered another way to burn calories that doesn't involve exercise or food. It's called involuntary isometrics in the dentist's chair. You see, I have PTSD from the sadistic dentist who drilled my teeth in 1958 without the benefit of a local anesthetic. Was it not available back then, or was he not trained to use it?

Well, I have a very competent, soft spoken dentist now who isn't stingy with the Novocain (or whatever it is they use), and a lovely dental assistant, who made my last two-hour stint not only bearable, but—well, I guess enjoyable would be a stretch. Truly, these wonderful professionals were a gift from God.

Anyway, their virtues don't mitigate my PTSD completely. Every one of the 600 muscles in my body go into spasm the second I hear the sound of the drill. I am careful not to show it—I don't want my dentist to feel bad. But let me tell you, two hours of isometric exercises must burn off a hell of a lot of calories.

All in all—a good day.

Shapewear

My goal is to be healthy and not have extra flesh that needs the latest shapewear (the modern word for girdles), to hold it in. I am not trying for the perfect body; but occasionally I would like to wear an outfit that doesn't have to double as camouflage.

I found a really pretty navy blue dress to wear to a wedding, with some bling at the neckline. It didn't have a waistline (that's key), and flattered my 70-year-old body—except for the slight bulge at the hips, revealed through the filmy, delicate fabric.

"You just need some shapewear and you'll be a knockout in this dress!" said the sales girl. What a sweetheart.

She directed me to the rows of elastic straitjackets. Hmm. Do I need tummy control or thigh control? Why don't they say hips? Oh—here's one that says it will hide bulges and ripples on my entire torso! I will look like Jennifer Lopez with this one.

I brought it into the dressing room and the struggle began. Don't the manufacturers know that the majority of women who buy these things are over 50 and dealing with arthritic joints and shoulder injuries? I yanked and pulled, nearly losing my balance and landing on the dressing room floor and then—finally, I looked like an hour glass with a purple face.

I reached for the dress, slid it over my squashed muscles and organs, and I must say, I think I did look like Jennifer Lopez. (What an imagination!)

And boy—the sales girl was making it big today—the dress that was on sale plus the shapewear that cost three times the amount of the dress. Excited to pay, I took off the dress and when I got to the straitjacket, I started to panic. I was locked in and couldn't maneuver my arms to yank the damn thing off. I sat down. I stood back up. I shimmied my shoulders. Sweat breaking out on my forehead, I considered calling for help.

I could see myself in one of those weird articles on my Internet home page, that try to lure you into reading the articles instead of checking your email. "Firefighters called to clothing store to save woman from unusual predicament." Then you have to scroll through 10 pages to see if the woman was burning up or trapped in her shapewear.

I struggled a bit longer, and after coming close to dislocating a hip and causing a tear in my shoulder's rotator cuff, I emerged from the dressing room, shapewear and dress in hand.

Why did I buy it? Because there's an old saying that it's painful to be beautiful.

After all, it was only one night. And I wanted to pretend I was J. Lo just once.

The Grandkids' Sports and Activities

Earlier in the book, I mentioned the crowded schedules the grandkids have these days. And because of that, we end up traveling to them rather than vice versa. New England soccer is brutal in the fall. Old Man Winter waits for us to show up for the October soccer games, and drops the temperature 20 degrees. On the Internet I saw a pop-up chair tent with zippered plastic windows that protect you from the wind during games. That was one smart entrepreneur who invented this. I wonder how many of his kids' games he sat through before he said, "Screw this. With my engineering degree, I am going to be warm—and rich."

Watching the kids' soccer games was a real learning curve. And it was harder to follow when they were 6-year-olds. They tore around the field like a bunch of scurrying, deranged termites, so not only was I in a fog as to what was happening—I could never find my grandchild.

It's definitely more exciting now that they are older, but I still don't know what it means to be "off-sides," even though a granddaughter drew lines in the sand and acted it out at the beach one day. I pretended I got it.

My favorite spectator sports are basketball and baseball—a nice warm gym and a sunny Little League field. Plus, I understand both games.

I played girls basketball from sixth grade till my sophomore year in high school, when I finally saw the handwriting on the wall that I wasn't going to bring the school a trophy. Apparently you needed to score more than two points a game. My skirted uniform never got a wrinkle, as I sat primly on the bench most of the game. I switched to theater, only to find I wasn't Broadway material either.

Our grandkids participate in almost every sport I've heard of: baseball, basketball, soccer, ice hockey, lacrosse (another hard one to figure out), gymnastics, track, horseback riding (that's a sport, right?).

One of our ten grandchildren chose music over sports, embracing everything I dreamed of doing as a child. She sings and dances with a wonderful stage presence, belting out songs from the musical *Annie* like a pro.

Even though our grandkids can't visit us as often as I'd like, I am delighted that they plunge in and take risks in their extra-curricular activities, knowing the value of the discipline it takes to excel while they are having fun.

My Garbage Disposal Guilt

###

A garbage disposal can be a tricky thing. One day it apparently choked when I stuffed too many apple peels down its throat in my hurry to get my pie into the oven. After trying the usual decloggers and boiling water, I had to call the plumber.

The second time I felt guilty. As Paul doesn't worry about expiration dates on perishables, and I do, I decided to hide the evidence of the raw sausage meat with the expired date on the package. I deposited it down the disposal, while he was at the gym. I felt sneaky, or worse, as if I was hiding a dead body, but the real guilt crept in when the water sat motionless in the sink, going nowhere. It ended with a plumber's visit and because I went to Catholic school, I felt I needed to confess to Paul.

"If we ate the damn sausage, it would have cost less to go to the hospital for food poisoning than the plumber's bill."

It's not that I look forward to visits from the plumber. Years later, after another kitchen clog, the plumber said, "Before I bring in my big machine with the snake, I will try to plunge it first."

"You're not using the same plunger you use for toilets, are you?"

"No Ma'am. I have a small one for sinks." He struggled without success and I saw him go out to the truck and come back with a bigger plunger...

Recently I narrowly escaped another plumbing bill. I was cleaning out my cabinets, and realized I had three 2-pound boxes of granulated sugar. I hardly ever use sugar, so whenever I'm in the store and get the idea to make something sweet, I never remember if I have any, so I buy a box.

Paul would never understand me throwing away perfectly good sugar, but the boxes were all open, I had no idea how old they were, and sugar is cheap; so it made perfect sense to dump the contents of two of the boxes down the garbage disposal. My mistake was not running hot water to dissolve the crystals before turning on the disposal switch. Instead of the usual crunching noise, all I heard was a dull hum. Oh my God, I broke it! What was I thinking???

I poured down boiling water (too late), turned on the switch and—nothing. I ran into the basement and flipped the circuit breaker switches and—nothing. Knowing I was going to hear the garage door opening any minute with Paul coming home from the barber, I called Lowe's Home Improvement store, which is programmed into my iPhone.

"Kitchen small appliances, please. And hurry."

"How may I help you, Ma'am?" After I explained my stupid maneuver, the salesman said I probably jammed it and there was a re-set button under the sink on the disposal.

"Ok, don't leave me until I find it," I yelled, after putting him on speaker and crawling under the sink.

"I don't see it!"

"It's small," he said. "See if you can feel it."

I ran my fingers over the circumference of the disposal, found the re-set button, and the wonderful, familiar crunching noise came back when I turned on the switch.

I am sure that was the first and last time he had a customer give him a virtual hug through the phone, just for telling her to push a button.

Unless you get the wrong impression, I really don't like to waste food. In fact, I choose to be the family's human guinea pig with many foods that fall into the gray area between edible and causing distressing GI symptoms. Yup, I will go down with the ship before wasting something that is questionable—especially if it's something I like. By the way, the smell test works only part of the time. There are some shifty little microbes that don't give you warning.

Sometimes, before I go to bed, I experiment with a bite of the eggplant parmesan leftovers that I lost track of in the refrigerator, or deli meat past the mysterious date stamped on the package. I figure it's only a few steps to the bathroom as opposed to experimenting during the day, and finding myself in Target when I collapse.

I've had good luck. But I'm not stupid either. There are times when my brain tells me to follow my mantra, "When in doubt—throw it out."

I Love Elephants

It seems that most Facebook posts are about grandchildren, politics, gardens, and golden retrievers. Every once in a while there's one about elephants. These very large animals have always fascinated me. Did you know that African elephants are the largest land animals on earth (many weighing 14,000 pounds), and they can live until the age of 70? If I had to drag 14,000 pounds around for 70 years, I would spend my life lounging under a baobab tree.

And their trunks—I would think it must be terribly annoying to have that thing flopping around in front of you 24 hours a day. Well, you probably know from watching nature shows that the elephant's trunk does *everything.* In fact, it's got about 40,000 muscles compared to 650 in the whole human body. An elephant also has a decent IQ, and if so inclined, it could probably knit you a sweater or do your car's next oil change with its trunk.

I learned to love elephants in the '50s, when we visited my grandparents in Pennsylvania. We always made a stop at the zoo. Keep in mind, this was before there were ethical laws to protect animals. Back then, sadly, they were housed in cages or large enclosures with outside space.

Anyway, I was introduced to Tillie, an elephant which was the pride of the city and the zoo. My grandfather would give me a handful of unshelled peanuts. The outside enclosure had two fences between Tillie and us, but she could lift her trunk over the bars to reach me and I would drop a peanut into her upturned trunk; then watch with glee as she pulled her trunk back and deposited the peanut into her mouth.

I mistakenly thought, after visiting today's more modern zoos, that elephants were quite satisfied with their new jungle-like surroundings—until I did some reading. A happy elephant needs miles to roam. Being very social (and sensitive) creatures, they also need the company of other elephants. There may come a point when we will have to go on a safari to see elephants in real life. While I have a new empathy for them, I'm grateful I got in under the wire to feed peanuts to Tillie, year after year. I had heard that elephants never forget, so I was sure she remembered me.

If you don't get your elephant fix on Facebook, there are lots of videos online. After watching them, I promise—you will want to give them a virtual hug.

Technology

###

remember reading in the newspaper when I was a teenager that future phones would have a screen that would allow you to see the person you were talking to. Such a cool idea. But what we didn't have, we didn't miss.

Every day I'd drag the rotary phone with its 12 foot cord into the coat closet, pull the door closed, make a space on the floor to sit in the dark between the snow boots—and talk about boys.

My parents didn't experience the tug of war our kids have with their kids, whose phones are just another appendage. I notice they confiscate their phones at 9 p.m. so they'll sleep, undistracted. Someone should confiscate mine when I go to bed.

FaceTime has brought our geographically spread out family together. It can be humbling, though. You can only blame the pandemic for so much. I see on the screen my gray roots and the frizz which I forgot to run a comb through. I need to be more careful. They'll be on their sibling text thread in no time and decide to have social services come check on us.

What's really mortifying is when my daughter says, "Mom, hold the phone out further. All I can see is the inside of your nose. And by the way, you might want to get out your little scissors."

One day while perched on the toilet, I must have hit FaceTime by mistake when I called my sister. My brother-in-law's face popped up on the screen. Aagh! I threw my phone across the floor, so all he could see was the ceiling. Thank God for "pocket dial."

Our kids think we need more and more technology. They gave us AirPods one year for Christmas. When I'm not losing them, I like them. I can get things done around the house while I'm talking on the phone.

Paul took a long walk one day and came home all upset that one of his AirPods must have fallen out of his ear. We both went out to re-trace his steps, staring at the grass along the sidewalk. We looked like two people with neck deformities, staring down to the left. No luck.

I have to give it to my husband—he is persistent. The next day he searched the route again.

"You are nuts," I said. "Didn't we just do this yesterday?" A half hour later, he showed up, triumphantly waving the AirPod in his hand.

This year we got the Amazon Echo/Alexa—Simon & Garfunkel and John Denver forever! Paul started getting tricky with it, and one day he told Alexa to call him in 45 minutes so he wouldn't be late for his dental appointment. When the alarm went off 45 minutes later, I heard him thanking her...

Sometimes he forgets her name and calls her Alexia, which she doesn't like. After the third time that he called her Alexia, I yelled from the other room, "Her name is Alexa!" Yep, Archie and Edith re-incarnated.

The other night we were watching a show on Netflix. All of a sudden Alexa started playing music. "Well, that's a little freaky," I said to Paul, until we realized one of the characters in the TV show called out to Alexa, his girlfriend, to play some music. We are now haunted by our new friend.

My First Zoom Meeting

###

Speaking of technology, during the pandemic I was invited to a Zoom meeting with my high school classmates. It was the first time I put lipstick on in weeks. (Paul has been saying I don't need makeup. I think his sight is starting to go.)

I got on Zoom at the appointed time, and saw my friends' faces, all with their lipstick and eye makeup in place—hands gesturing, but no sound.

"I'm here," I said. "Can you hear me?" I asked with my fingers pointing to my ears. I tried to lip read, which didn't work—they were talking too fast. I couldn't tell if they could see me, so I started to click everything on the screen. That's always my big mistake. Apparently, during my crazed clicking, I subscribed to a tech support service that later took me three hours to cancel.

As I'm trying to figure out the lack of sound, I got a text from one of my friends. "We can't hear you or see you. All that pops up is your name."

Getting frustrated, I yelled for Paul. He pulled the desk and computer away from the wall and started checking the plugs, while I went in and out of Zoom, waving to my friends, pointing at my ears, and texting, "Still trying."

I have no idea what he did, but next thing I knew—they were complementing Paul on his new beard. Already 25 minutes into the Zoom gathering, I had the nerve to say, "Ok, tell me what I missed."

"You didn't really ask that, did you?"

At the end of the meeting, someone asked if I wanted to organize the next meeting, which was quickly voted down by the others.

The next week I got on early to avoid the mess. Same thing happened. Paul pulled the desk and computer away from the wall again, but this time without success. I told him to forget it and go back to watching his show on TV. I would tinker around with it and if I got on, I got on.

I looked behind the computer and was shocked to see at least 10 wires and/or cables running in a tangled mess from the computer and printer to surge protectors on the floor—so disturbing to my minimalist mind.

Please tell me why a laptop has only one cord?

Anyway, no wonder I couldn't get on Zoom—probably a loose connection. I must have worked the magic that Paul did the previous week, as all of a sudden, their voices came through at an ear drum blasting volume, and everybody could see me.

After 10 minutes of talking about our gray pandemic roots, it was time to go.

The Nice Policeman in Rehoboth

#

I have never been good with directions. If you spin me around once, I no longer know what city I'm in. I never won "Pin the Tail on the Donkey." The collage of family pictures on the wall next to the donkey poster always got the tail.

I've read these incredible stories of blindfolded kidnap victims who are whisked away in the back seat of a car, who track the ride and mentally construct a map in their brain. Lordy, you can all say goodbye to me right now. After 10 minutes, my panicked mind will already have me three states away.

As you know, I *love* my GPS navigational system. However, I did have an unfortunate incident and I needed a very nice policeman to get me out of the mess. I was driving south on Rt.1 in Delaware to a destination I had programmed into my iPhone's GPS. Rt.1 has crossovers in the median that cars on either side of the highway can use to change their direction. My phone said to turn left in a half mile. I got in the left lane and saw one of those crossovers. The problem—it was only a quarter mile, and this particular egress was ONLY for the cars traveling north in the opposite direction. Are you still following me?

Anyway, I pulled into the median, only to realize I was staring into the eyeballs of a man in the car coming towards me (legally, I might add) and beeping his horn.

My mind went blank. Do I back up into the heavy traffic going south, or make hand motions to the angry driver that I was sorry and didn't know what to do. And then I saw the familiar flashing blue lights. With a sick feeling, I knew I was headed for the county jail—in hand cuffs. How I let my family down!

Out of the squad car came a young, handsome cop who approached my car. Almost in tears, I started babbling, "I don't know what happened, Officer. I was following my GPS and…"

He held up his hand to stop the traffic behind me and said, "Don't worry Ma'am—just back up and get yourself in the left lane again."

"Thank you, Officer. God bless you."

I was back in the left lane, angering drivers on both sides of the road. And then I figured out the mistake I made. I should have turned in a half mile, not a quarter—at a red light in a big intersection.

I don't know if he treated me with kid gloves because it was Christmas, or because I reminded him of his flaky grandmother. If I hadn't caused such havoc, I would have asked him for a selfie.

My Mother Never Told Me

I couldn't wait to have kids, and after the four of them came, I loved each one. However—I had a revelation. My mother didn't tell me everything.

You see, I imagined a peaceful *Leave It to Beaver* kind of life ahead of me. Mom, were you afraid I would ditch the whole parenting thing if you gave me the entire picture? Like, how toddlers don't like naps; how siblings argue, tattle, and inflict bodily harm on each other; how whining and the constant refrain of "I'm bored" fill in the blanks. And here's the big one—how sleep deprived I would be with my colicky baby (actually—how sleep deprived I would be until the last one left for college).

Don't get me wrong—I was very happy being a mother. And I have albums of pictures where I had genuine smiles to prove it. I just needed to acquire coping mechanisms (other than alcohol) to deal with the realities my mother never told me about.

Oh, and to learn how to say the powerful and inspirational directive to my children, "If you are bored, use your imagination. Alexander Graham Bell probably invented the telephone because he was bored. Think how proud he made his mother."

We didn't have a lot of electronics back then, with the exception of Atari, Mario brothers, and Pacman—which might have been a good thing. We didn't raise an Alexander Graham Bell, but our kids did follow their own dreams as they grew up.

My mother also never told me how my heart would ache when our children took turns getting rejected by a friend.

She never told me how hard it would be to watch the high school basketball coach keep Sharon and Eleanor, our two oldest, on the bench—putting them in the game for the last 45 seconds, even though they were ahead by 20.

And she never told me how my stomach would knot, my heart would rip apart, and my tears would flow when they were sick, sad, or lying on an emergency room gurney.

A little segue—when Brian fell off his new bike and cut his chin, we were in the ER when the doctor asked me to step out of the room while he stitched up the laceration. I told him I would like to stay, as I was a nurse and I'd be OK. He then firmly repeated his request for me to step out of the room. I felt my face on fire, and stomped out into the hallway, afraid that if I resisted and caused a scene, Brian might get hysterical.

He actually did quite well. When Brian asked the doctor if he needed stitches, the doctor said, "No—you only need sutures." He pulled one over on him, but it worked. I know I should let it go, but I still get mad as hell, 40 years later, when I remember pacing in the hall, outside the treatment room.

And it doesn't end. Watching *adult* children suffer from anything, big or small, and knowing all you can do is listen and pray, adds another reality. They are your children forever.

Now we have grandchildren. I had no idea that I would have such strong feelings for these little extensions of their parents. And whenever anything bad happens to them, I get a double whammy. The heart wrenching feelings return, not just for the grandchild, but also for the parent, my grown-up child, because I know exactly how they feel.

Now, I know this book probably appeals mostly to post-menopausal women, but if you are of childbearing age and you are considering having a child, you probably just broke out in a sweat. So—go wipe off your forehead, have a cookie (or a glass of wine), and then come back to read the rest.

Waiting...

Feeling better now? Keep this in mind. The positives drown out the negatives. Really—they do. I had to sit here pulling things out of my memory to write what my mother never told me. And I'm glad she didn't. It's true that my heart rips in two on occasion, but more often than not, it's bursting with joy.

Paul, the Car, and Me

We bought a new car that has a keyless ignition and a key fob. Whoever thought up this nutty idea of ditching the key, obviously did not have aging neurons in their brain.

"I don't know what the big deal is," said my husband. "Just keep the key fob on or near your body all the time." It's been a learning curve, but I'm OK now, with a pink, coiled, pony tail holder around my wrist holding my dangling key fob.

I felt like Captain Sully Sullenberger, when I looked at the dashboard. Car manufacturers don't understand that some of us are minimalists. It was touch and go on the highway for the first week, pressing the wrong buttons. Good thing I was in a parking lot when I pressed the button to turn off the ignition instead of the radio.

For the first two weeks, every time I made a turn, the windshield wiper fluid started squirting after I *thought* I turned on the blinker. And if that's not startling enough, a horn would blare from the car behind me.

I'm also not crazy about the navigational system on the dash— too much information with small letters and arrows popping up. My iPhone's GPS is just fine. Nice and simple and I like her voice better.

Paul and I are the dynamic duo on car trips, though our kids refer to us as Seinfeld's parents. As I said earlier, Archie and Edith Bunker would be more accurate.

On a recent trip to Washington, DC, Paul was following the GPS on the dashboard of the new car. And I had *my* iPhone in my hand, with the GPS up and running for added assurance. Yep, 2 GPS's going simultaneously—and we still missed the turn. As we were barreling down the Rock Creek Parkway with no exit in site, the excited GPS ladies were screeching "Recalculating—recalculating!" Then one told us to make a U-turn while the other wanted us to take the next exit.

"I told you we should have followed my iPhone directions," was followed by Archie Bunker yelping, "Turn that effin thing off before we crash through the concrete barriers at the White House."

Oh yes, we work so well together—the dynamic duo.

Our home in Delaware has a very narrow garage, and it takes skill to maneuver two cars inside without ripping off one of the mirrors. The new car was a tiny bit wider, so I got daily reminders from Paul to be careful going out (as well as to watch the neighbor's mailbox behind me across the street).

Well, one day the side view mirror of my car got ripped off, and guess what—it wasn't me! Boy—did I ever silently scream with glee as I consoled my embarrassed husband.

Speaking of mirrors, that message imprinted on the side view mirrors always confuses me—"Objects in mirror are closer than they appear." While I'm passing a 16-wheeler, I try and remember—objects in mirror are *larger* or *closer* than they appear? And is the truck larger or closer in my *side view* mirror or my *rear view* mirror? So I slow up while I figure this out as I hear Paul screaming, "Step on it! What the heck are you doing?"

I don't know why the vehicle you're trying to pass can't look the same in both mirrors. Somebody dropped the ball on this one.

Just a bit of trivia—don't park too close to the garage wall, because even though you are proud that you can slither your body out through the narrow space, the physics are different when you get back in and you could decapitate yourself.

Nervous Laughter

I remember kneeling in the pews of St Ursula's Church with my third-grade class, covering my mouth with my hands as a classmate and I tried to stifle giggles each time we locked eyes. I'm sure the nun sitting behind us could see our bodies shaking in unison.

It still happens. The most distressing time was the day I met my sister Betsy, to bid farewell to our dying father in the hospital. We pressed the elevator button to go up to the 7th floor, where my mother was waiting for us at his bedside. We were stressed, and nervous, and sad at the prospect of his impending death. And what did we do? Both of us broke out in muffled, nervous giggling while waiting for the elevator. The more we tried to stop, the more we giggled. I finally made myself have a fit of coughing, in case anyone we knew happened to walk by. Halfway up to the seventh floor, as sadness set in, our faces portrayed the beginnings of grief.

I recently Googled nervous laughter. Apparently, it's a thing—and not a bad thing. You can't help it and it acts as a defense mechanism to handle anxiety caused by sad or traumatic events. Whew! So relieved to know we weren't being disrespectful to my dear father.

The Cheesecake

###

I copied a wonderful cheesecake recipe from a newspaper years ago, when we lived for a short time in upstate New York. It was the chef's masterpiece from the Hotel Syracuse. I'm still surprised that he shared it. How could it not be good, with a dozen eggs, a ton of butter, sour cream, cream cheese, and heavy cream. Yes, I know—too much saturated fat. But, the idea is—to have a delicate little piece and savor it.

I bought a special cheesecake pan and after filling it with the cheesecake batter, placed it in a water bath (which is a roasting pan filled with a couple inches of water).

It was in the oven forever, it seemed, and the top turned to a golden brown. I went to take it out, and it started to jiggle. I didn't understand—it should have been done. I was making it for company, and I wasn't about to screw this up. So I did what I do best—I grabbed the phone. Calling the chef at the Hotel Syracuse, I asked him why my cheesecake was still jiggling. He said it should be done and that when it settled it would congeal to a solid. What a guy!

It finally stopped jiggling, and after a few hours in the refrigerator, we ate a creamy slice of heaven.

Years later, I had people over during the holidays for hors d'oeuvres and dessert. Even though everyone offered to bring something, I said they didn't need to. I had fun preparing my favorite canapes and the cheesecake was going to cap the evening. One of our guests brought a chocolate cream pie. I placed it in the refrigerator, making a mental note to make sure I served my cheesecake before everybody filled themselves up with the chocolate pie.

A few guests had to leave early, before dessert, and after I escorted them to the door, I came back into the kitchen to see the chocolate cream pie making its way to the table. NOOO! I whipped out the cheesecake from the refrigerator, telling myself to go slow, so I wouldn't trip and fall, with my face buried in the creamy concoction of expensive ingredients. I didn't need to worry. The cheesecake was a hit. And so was the chocolate cream pie. And, that's okay.

Husbands

Sometimes I have to swallow hard and smile. I married my soulmate, not a clone of myself. And that's a good thing. I like to think we are complementary, and on the same page with most of the important stuff.

I used to think I was a planner. Well, now that Paul's impulsivity has cooled down in retirement, *he* has turned into the planner. From discussing at dinner the time we should leave for church the next morning to get a good parking space, to planning his next headache—he's the best.

In all fairness, I am pretty good at planning my next headache, too. However, I am terrible at making plans. I kind of envy people who know exactly where they are going to be on September 8th a year from now. What holds me back is the thought of breaking a plan if something else comes up that is a priority in my brain.

I drive Paul crazy with this rationale. "Just say yes and if there's an emergency, we'll cancel!"

"I don't think our friends are going to consider the tournament finals of our grandkid's soccer team an emergency." Of course, during the pandemic, breaking plans became more common than making plans.

Another difference between us is that I overthink. Everything is a physics problem. Add Google to the mix for research, and I may come up with a solution before the world ends.

I wish my dear husband, though, would overthink occasionally. Back in the '70s (so he gets a pass for being young), we had some of his family over for dinner. Our old fashioned dining room had a hutch with my grandmother's china on the shelves. After dinner, I asked Paul to give his sister and her husband coffee while I got dessert. After they left and we were clearing the table, I realized that instead of getting the cups from inside the cabinet, he gave them the coffee cups that were for *show* on the hutch with a year's worth of dust inside. Funny they didn't notice it floating on top of the coffee.

My aunt was right with the old proverb, "You have to eat a peck of dirt before you die."

My Missing Handbag

###

Have you ever left something on the roof of your car because you were juggling three things plus an umbrella while trying to open the car door? Well, the something I left on the roof was my handbag. I drove to my writers' group gathering, and as I got out of the car I realized instantly that something was missing. I searched the back seat and the trunk only to get that sick feeling in the pit of my stomach, realizing that my handbag was lying somewhere on the 10 miles of road I had just driven on.

Dusk had turned into darkness and I now had to retrace my route, alternately turning my high beams on and off as oncoming traffic approached. Squinting into the lights and going 25 mph, my hands gripped the wheel as I scanned the road shoulder and ditches—unsuccessfully.

"You didn't stay long at the writers' group," Paul said.

After he heard what happened, we both jumped back into the car. "I already searched the side of the road," I said. "We're not going to find it. Someone probably stole it by now."

"You look while I drive."

A half hour later, I was calling banks and credit card companies, and after getting assurances that no one had yet used my cards, I put a temporary hold on them. Maybe in the daylight I would find it had flown into the field where I made that sharp turn—too fast.

An hour later, while on Facebook, an instant message popped up. A kind soul tracked me down, because he saw a purse lying in the road, and he retrieved my wallet full of credit cards and $40 in cash. (Come to think of it, that was such a guy move. A woman would have scooped up the purse as well.) Anyway, he was traveling on business and told me the name of the hotel he was staying at 15 miles away. Hallelujah! There are still good people in this world.

Just in case I was wrong, and he wasn't such a kind soul, Paul came with me to retrieve my wallet. He met us in the lobby and turned out to be a very sweet man, and of course I gave him the $40 that was still in the wallet.

I never did find my purse with my sunglasses that were probably crushed to smithereens. I got a new pair of glasses out of the deal, so it all ended well.

Vertebrae and Funerals

###

I get the purpose of speed bumps, as they've kept me from a few speeding tickets and also from harming others. However, while on vacation, we went to a church in Florida that had a very long access road, with multiple speed bumps. I think whoever installed them made the bumps a tad higher than they needed to be. If any of the parishioners had any lumbar spine issues, their vertebrae got rearranged by the time they made it to the front door. I mean—how many old, retired people speed on church property? We are headed to pray for our souls, not to a sale at Macy's.

Speaking of getting older, we have been to a rash of funerals this past year. And sadly, they were close relatives and friends. We came to the realization that we are not ready to die. Well, to be more accurate, we've made no plans.

"You've made no plans?" asked one of our adult kids. "How are we supposed to know what cemetery to put you in?"

After the last funeral, Paul decided we better get down to business. He said, "It's not fair to the kids. We need to make a new will, as the last will has the four of them going to your deceased mother, should we both die." Of course, our kids are all well into adulthood now. But, by the time this book gets published, we will probably have everything in order and tied up in a bow, from cremation or burial (don't have that answer yet), the church and the chosen hymns, and the state and cemetery where we'll rest our bones. Last but not least, we need to plan the funeral luncheon.

Do we have a buffet, or a sit-down luncheon? Do we have breakfast food or dinner food? At one recent funeral repast (I heard it's called that with those in the know), they had a combination of both. Eggs

Benedict *and* chicken picatta—I felt like I died and went to heaven. (Sorry—couldn't resist.)

I don't know what it is about my stomach. No matter how sad I am, I never lose my appetite at funerals. Maybe it's because I have faith that our dear ones are in a better place, because I enjoy every morsel of the chicken parmesan, baked cod, and ziti on my plate. I even eat the roll, which for me is just a vehicle for the soft butter, because nothing is better than butter. I figure that the grieving process will use up the calories.

My next book might be how to organize a memorable funeral. Keep in mind, a quarter of my blood is Irish.

What's Therapy for Some Is Torture for Others

###

I would come home from the hospital at the end of my shift—my mind weary from the emotion of the day and the constant mental concentration that demanded accuracy when administering IV medications and monitoring critical lab reports. I was always on the alert for the subtle signs that a patient was about to quickly deteriorate.

Seeing a pile of clean laundry on the bed after I got home was not the turn-off that you might expect. After showering and getting into my sweats, I would absentmindedly begin to fold, with my mind drifting off to nothingness. What therapy this was for my spirit.

I think that mindless tasks are occasionally good for the soul. Is it possible that this form of mindlessness could be a form of *mindfulness*? I know—sounds confusing. I need to ask my friend, who is an expert on this topic. There is just something about folding towels that calms me.

We had an elderly, agitated patient one day at the hospital who was a challenge. I asked her if she could help me fold washcloths. She looked at me quizzically as I walked her to a chair next to the desk where I was charting on my other patients. I placed a pile of rumpled, clean washcloths on the tray table in front of her. As she picked up each one, a visible calm settled over her fragile body. One washcloth after another was folded in half, then in half again, into a perfect square. She either reverted back to her days as a 1950's housewife, or she was a geometry teacher who wanted her 90-degree angles to be perfect.

Years later, I was telling this story to our daughter, an accomplished artist. She looked at me—horrified. I forgot that laundry is on her hate list.

"Mom, I will lose it if anyone ever asks me to fold washcloths in the nursing home when I'm old."

"Don't worry, honey. When they see that look on your face, they'll remember the pencils and sketch pad that your children brought in for that very reason."

I Stuffed My Last Turkey

###

Would you like a little tip to reduce the stress of your next Thanksgiving dinner? I saw a recipe on the Internet for stuffing made in the crockpot, with a lot of good reviews (I always check the reviews). I decided I would try it at our daughter's house one Thanksgiving. I was in charge of the turkey for the non-vegetarian part of the family.

Midmorning, after shooing the late sleepers who were getting breakfast out of the kitchen, I started the fight with the cold, greasy, 20-pound bird—trying to pull out the gizzards that always seem to be frozen inside the "fresh" turkey.

I was excited at the thought of using a crockpot for the stuffing. It would remove the logistical stress of getting the stuffing ingredients assembled in a timely manner and deposited into the cavern of this hefty, featherless fowl so it could finally make its way into the oven.

My sister was bringing the creamed onions and mashed sweet potatoes with toasted marshmallows on top (Thanksgiving staples since we were children). Loving tradition, she pleaded with me to stuff the turkey, so I agreed, sort of—half the stuffing in the turkey and half in the crockpot. It was a good experiment, and I must say, the crockpot stuffing was really, really good. So, sorry dear sister, but I don't think I will ever stuff a turkey again. Maybe in the future, we'll come to your house for Thanksgiving, where tradition reigns.

The Martian

###

When I am stressed, I pace, eat, pray, and eat some more. A few years ago, I got a call from our daughter, Eleanor. "I feel like my head is going to explode." I hoped it was just one of her migraines, and not something more sinister.

"Oh, sorry honey. Call me later and let me know how you are."

Then Annie called on the way to the oral surgeon, post wisdom tooth extraction, with alveolar osteitis, other-wise known as "dry socket." It only occurs in a small percent of patients, but is very painful.

"Oh, sorry honey. Call me when you get home and tell me what they did for you."

Then my dear husband said, "Mary Ann, let's you and I go see *The Martian.* It's playing over in Midway Cinemas." He has the inordinate ability to put everything into little boxes in his brain until further notice—a true example of living in the moment.

"Are you crazy? How can you go to the movies after I just told you about these two phone calls?"

"So you're going to pace for three hours? We might as well go see a movie. Just bring your cell phone along and put it on vibrate."

He had a point. And since we only go to the movies about twice a year, I figured I couldn't say no. Plus, if I had something to concentrate on, I wouldn't have my head in the refrigerator looking for something to eat.

I realized as we pulled into the parking lot that I had 5 percent battery left on my phone. Lovely.

I did get engrossed in the movie, though. I mean—Matt Damon stuck on Mars all by himself, possibly until he died, if no one rescued him! It catapulted my anxiety up ten more notches. Way to go, Paul.

We touched base with our two daughters on the way home. Eleanor's head was still intact, albeit with a bad migraine. Her medicine, strong coffee, and dark bedroom were keeping the pain at bay.

Annie's oral surgeon packed her empty tooth socket with numbing medication.

The next voice in my ear was Paul. "See—the world is still turning. And you didn't gain a pound, since you couldn't raid the refrigerator for three hours."

"Thank you for pointing that out."

Perks to Having Creaky Joints

Occasionally, when the regular stalls in the women's public restroom looked like the cleaning crews called out sick, I would check out the handicapped stall. If the bathroom was empty, I'd sneak in and go quickly before I got caught, or worse, had to look into the face of a bent over, frail, 90-year-old as I emerged. You know my feelings about public restrooms. Well, I love the wide open space in the stalls made for wheelchairs and walkers, so I can make my bird's nest of toilet paper to line the seat without my elbow or head banging into anything germy. Plus, they usually have their own sink.

One day, when I was being good and went into one of the smaller stalls for healthy skeletons, I panicked when I tried to get up. The toilet seat felt like it was three inches from the floor. Damn—did they put a child's toilet in here? I can't get up! The thought of having to ask the next restroom visitor for assistance, or worse, to call 911, made me gather all my thigh muscle strength and pop up like a surface-to-air missile.

Now, finally, I can legally go into the handicapped bathroom with the higher toilet seat. The problem is, I don't look handicapped. Maybe I could get a copy of my x-ray films and tape it to the outside of the stall door before I go in.

The fact is, my insides look a lot worse than my outsides, so everybody would probably think I stole the films from my mother.

Or, maybe I could carry a foldable cane in my handbag, but that wouldn't seem honest. Remember, I went to Catholic school.

The Pandemic (continued)

###

I laugh now at everybody wiping door handles and grocery carts with antiseptic wipes. Welcome to my OCD world. I could have used a little more humor when I struggled with this lovely affliction 40 years ago. Of course, it will always be a part of me, but it no longer controls me, thanks to therapy, medication, prayer, and—you guessed it, humor. Apparently, I need to get comfortable with uncertainty (according to some really great self-help books).

One thing I've learned, while following the shelter-in-place guidelines, is how true the old adage is—"Never put off 'til tomorrow what you can do today." After all, a pandemic could be just around the corner. For eight years we've been procrastinating about changing the look of our guest bedroom.

"I *knew* we should have gotten the walls painted last year. I know the exact color I want so it matches the new bedspread, but now we have to wait until after the pandemic for a painter to work in our house."

"I told you I can do this, Mary Ann," stated my husband.

"Honey, I don't care what you told me. We have the high ceiling in that room and you're too old to be climbing a ladder that tall. And Home Depot isn't an essential trip. We've waited eight years. What's one more?"

Speaking of essential trips, I used to enjoy going to the grocery store that's just around the corner. I'd go in for pork chops and end up hanging out in the Hallmark card aisle. And since I'm a marketer's dream, I'd leave the store with the newest shade of L'Oreal blush and the latest twist on salted caramel ice cream.

Now, my weekly essential trip to the grocery store is a dreaded work in progress. It was helpful when they made the aisles *one way* and painted arrows on the floor for people like me. Trouble is, I forget to look down. I walk fast to begin with, and now with the pandemic, I walk faster in the grocery store to get the hell out quick. Last week, I nearly caused a 10 cart pileup by racing in the wrong direction, as I was about to round a corner. Everyone seemed impressed with my quick reflexes in making a U-turn.

Then the grocery store started requiring that everyone wear a mask. Remember that refreshing feeling we used to get after a hearty sneeze? Well, it's sure not the same with a mask. But it keeps people from fainting around you.

The graphic images of the coronavirus you see on TV and on the Internet are actually kind of pretty, resembling clusters of red roses popping out of a miniature gray tennis ball. And get this—if you are infected, they float in the air when you talk or sing. I can't get that image out of my mind every time I hear Andrea Bocelli belt out a song, spewing tiny tennis balls covered in roses into the air.

Until I got my cute masks that I ordered online, I was wearing my home-made mask fashioned out of a pillow case from instructions I found on the Internet. I proudly sent a photo to our kids and was told it looked like a diaper. I guess that's why nobody could hear me in the grocery store when I asked a question; and probably why I was gasping for breath by the time I left, with everybody running from me as if I had the virus. By the way, to my fellow shoppers—a mask doesn't cover your eye rolls.

Thankfully, Paul and I have been healthy. Although, in late May of 2020, Paul started with the sniffles and tearing of his eyes. COVID-19 alarm bells went up. Thermometer came out—no fever. Whew, that was close. Tree and grass pollen levels were high, so I told Paul it sounded like it was allergies. I de-pollenated the house with my vacuum and Swiffered the hardwood floors. I went the extra mile, laundering the sheets and quilt. Last, I washed all his CPAP tubings.

"You're good to go now, Paul. Not one granule of pollen anywhere in the house." The next day the sneezing continued. Damn! Maybe he does have a cold. But how the hell did he get it? We've been sheltering in place for weeks. He had a miraculous turn for the better a few days later, so I guess we'll never know.

I'm glad we didn't need to see a doctor for any perceived emergencies. That is, until poor Paul got an ingrown toe nail. We ignored it for a while—thinking maybe the nail would make a 90 degree turn and grow out, instead of in. We soaked it in salt water. Why am I saying *we*? Maybe because we are very romantic and do these unromantic things together. Or maybe it's the nurse in me. "Are we ready for our Fleets enema?"

His toe started to get red. Again, we procrastinated too long. The podiatrist was all booked up with pandemic foot emergencies, but scheduled a teleconference. The office said we could use an iPhone, which was an interesting experience. As I was on my hands and knees FaceTiming Paul's big toe, I could hear the doctor yelling multiple times, "All I see is the carpet."

At the same time (I told you we do things together), when I flossed my teeth one day, my gums started to bleed (sorry). Oh my God, I have gingivitis! And it's all my fault, with my pandemic laziness—occasionally forgetting to floss. I got on the Internet and googled how to fix gingivitis at home, and began flossing twice a day, brushing three times, and rinsing with salt water in between.

With all the sodium chloride I was dumping into Paul's foot soaks for his ingrown toenail and my salt water rinses to bring back my healthy gums, I needed to buy a lot of Morton's salt when I went to the store. If anybody was watching, I bet they grabbed a few, too, thinking there must be a salt shortage, just like the toilet paper. And that's how panic buying starts.

During the pandemic, we sat home and watched Mass online from the comfort of our sofas. I like a good homily, the new word for sermon in church. A few humorous jokes are always good, because I believe that God laughs. Without feedback from a live congregation, some of the jokes fell flat, to our good-natured pastor's chagrin.

I'm so glad the homilies aren't hell fire and brimstone anymore. In my opinion, the best ones exude God's love—and most importantly, are short and succinct. I'm a daydreamer, and unless the priest is God himself, my mind starts to drift after 10 minutes. I keep reining in my thoughts only to have them sneak in another direction.

Now that I'm 70, I really should have more discipline. When I'd look at the pious faces around me, they seemed rapt in concentration, hanging onto every word. Of course, for all I know, they were trying to decide which dress to return to Marshalls after Mass.

At home when I pray, just like in church, my thoughts are often like butterflies on speed. So, sometimes I have props to keep me focused.

I light a candle. That helps. And sometimes I listen to the Ave Maria sung by Josh Groban on my AirPods. I turn the volume way up and feel like I'm in heaven. I'll probably need to ask the kids for a hearing aid this Christmas.

Time for a COVID break. Keep smiling. To be continued…

Another Dog Story

As you know, our children all have dogs. Having never been a dog person, I'm surprised how much I look forward to visiting our kids along with their canines. They all have big dogs, except for our oldest. Sharon's family has a little Havanese. The kids think that we need a puppy. If we did get a dog, (and we're not), I would have a little dog like Sharon's—one that sits on your lap and has tiny poops. But we get our dog fix when we visit each family, so I think we're good.

We doggie-sit the big one, occasionally, when the kids visit us in Delaware. She's a rescue dog—a mix with mostly American Staffordshire Terrier (fancy name, huh?). Not only is she lovable—she never barks.

I used to have one rule—that the dogs couldn't lie on the sofas or beds. I enforced this with as much consistency as I did with the rules I gave our kids years ago. I was a pushover then and I finally crumbled with the dogs.

We doggie-sat Bella for three days a few months ago. Annie informed us, "Just throw an old quilt on the floor in your bedroom at night, and she'll sleep on that." Popping into my mind was the memory of Paul's CPAP tubing flailing in the wind when Bella jumped up on the bed as a puppy.

"We'll see how it works, Paul. Don't worry. If she acts up, I'll bring her into the living room and close the door." Bedtime came and I arranged the quilt on the floor, and put some crunchy dog treats on top.

"C'mon, Bella. Night-night time." She obediently stepped onto her makeshift bed on the floor and started eating her treats. Paul and I got into bed and we didn't move a muscle. All I could hear was the faint rhythmic whishing of the CPAP machine. I heard Bella starting to scrooch around on the blanket, but— like a little baby, I figured she was just settling herself.

Next thing I knew, it was three in the morning, and I heard the sound of her toenails on the hardwood floor with a sad little whine every few minutes. "Do you think she needs to go out and pee?" I whispered to Paul. He took off his face paraphernalia, put on his sneakers, and off they went into the back yard.

We settled ourselves back in the bed a second time, but this time Bella wasn't on board with the quilt on the floor. After a few minutes of pacing, I knew she was thinking, "Oh heck, what do I have to lose. If they don't want me on the bed, they can freak out and I'll be back on the floor."

Yep, I was right. She popped up and lay on the end of our bed, curled around our feet. "I guess I'm okay with it if you're okay, Paul." He was already asleep.

The morning sun peaked through the shades and I figured that Bella probably didn't feel welcome in our bed, as I no longer felt the warm mass hovering at my feet. I rolled over to tell Paul, and found I was staring into two big black eyes that didn't belong to my husband. Without us ever suspecting, Bella wiggled her big body into the narrow space between Paul and me! I didn't know whether I should be flattered or horrified. I have to say, I did feel warm and cozy when I woke up. Boy, have I come a long way—though I did decide to throw my sheets in the laundry.

The following morning at 6 o'clock, Paul took her out to pee while I was still sleeping. The noise of his stomping feet headed back to our bedroom woke me up. Next thing I knew, he charged through the door, screaming, "Bella's lost. She ran away!"

"You didn't put her on a leash?"

"I couldn't find it and I didn't want to wake you."

"Oh my God, how are we gonna tell the kids?" I cried as we went out to the back deck.

It was pitch black out, being December, and we couldn't see a thing. Both of us started yelling "Bella!"

Out of nowhere, she appeared like a vision and ran right back into the house, without so much as an "I'm sorry for giving you a heart attack."

As I mentioned earlier, this housing development has no backyard barriers. With her night vision, Bella must have thought in her dog brain, "Hot damn—a football field with no fences!"

Absconding With the Phone Chargers

###

"**M**ake sure we have all our chargers," is Paul's refrain each time we are packing up to go home from a visit with the kids and their families; and vice versa, whenever they leave our house.

Before he got started with this ritual reminder, we used to hunt for our phone chargers under sofa cushions, in the car, in my handbag—finally resorting to blaming each other for petty theft.

On subsequent visits to their houses, I'd see Paul eyeing a charger cord, and a second later ask, "Mary Ann, isn't that your phone charger that we couldn't find last month?" He's gotten very obsessive about his own cord. He knows where it is at all times.

Even though there are chargers all over the houses of our kids, I would frequently hear, "Grandma, could I borrow your charger over night? I promise I'll give it back in the morning." She'd be out the door to catch the school bus before I woke up and next thing I knew we were on the road back to Delaware. The charger cord—attached to the wall outlet in her bedroom.

"I found a long, fluorescent pink charging cord in Walmart," I announced to Paul one day. "I'll never lose my cord again."

"No, I disagree. It will only work if you remember to run through all the kids' bedrooms looking for a pink cord."

Tax Season

###

I don't like anything to do with numbers. That includes our bank account, our investments, our bills, the car's speedometer, and our bathroom scale.

I prefer words. I know I need numbers in my life to exist, and I should be grateful for our investments that may very well determine if the nursing home I go to someday serves wine.

Paul, on the other hand, loves numbers. I must say he's been a good planner, and knows where every penny goes—even to the last time I was in CVS, thanks to the Internet. "Was that $34.99 for medicine or make-up? Gotta know these things for the IRS."

This year's resolution is to get up to speed on money matters. I can't count on being the first to go, and I'm not a quick learner when it comes to finances. Just so you don't think I'm completely irresponsible, I do know how to balance our check book —the old fashioned way, with a paper register.

Watching Paul work on the taxes this year was painful. Even though our taxes were filed on the computer, he had forms spread all over the kitchen table. He was telling me something about selling stock to buy a car and the IRS needed to know the gains and my eyes started glazing over. I told him that if he goes suddenly, before I learn all this, I am calling an accountant. I'll direct him to our over-stuffed file cabinet and give him all the passwords he needs to break into our computer files.

"It's all yours," I'll say, "and I want you to take all of my money out of every account so I can keep it under my mattress." Paul's eyes start bulging and he breaks out in hives whenever I say that. And to any thieves reading this, you realize this is just a book.

Reading Glasses

Before I tell you about my reading glasses, I have to say that my eyes are not normal. Not that anybody's eyes are normal after the age of 40, but I have multiple issues. I'm not ready for a guide dog yet, thanks to modern medicine. By the way, if you need your cataracts out, it's a piece of cake. Instilling the endless eye drops before and after cataract surgery is the only annoying part. I administered eye drops to tons of patients when I worked in the hospital. But giving them to myself—I kept missing my eye. And those eye drop bottles are so tiny; they don't hold a lot of liquid. With my nursing background, I would have been mortified to tell the doctor I ran out of drops because I couldn't find my eye.

After the surgery, I only needed glasses for reading which he said I could get at the drug store. I bought one pair, which was a mistake. I kept losing them all over the house.

"Paul, I've looked everywhere that I could possibly have placed my glasses. This is so frustrating!"

"Yes, you looked everywhere except the top of your head."

I'm thinking of getting one of those cords to wear around my neck to hold my glasses. I saw a pretty beaded one online that looks like a necklace. I've resisted because I thought it would make me look like a grandmother. And yes, I know what you're going to say.

My poor near vision is really not a big deal unless I'm on the phone with a credit card company and they want me to read off the numbers on my card; or if I want to make sure it's ibuprofen I'm taking, and not Paul's heart pill.

Plastic Straws

I get the whole thing about ruining the environment and killing fish with plastic. But most of you know my solution. Surely it's just a matter of time before an MIT graduate figures out how to burn everything up, including plastic, and filter all the bad stuff from the smoke. Why is that so difficult? Ashes to ashes. Dust to dust. Garbage and trash would be one and the same.

I used to drink everything with a straw. I'd even stick one in a can of beer, to Paul's chagrin. The first time I tried a paper straw, I was sipping a Bloody Mary at a Florida restaurant. My lips stuck to the cardboard. I was debating whether to rub some of my lip gloss on the top of the straw, but nobody else seemed to be having a problem. I figured maybe they're like chop sticks and you just have to get used to them.

I was introduced to metal straws at our daughter's home. "How in God's name do you clean these?" I asked Sharon. "I doubt the spray in your dishwasher can reach up into those things and get rid of the dried up strawberry yogurt shake that's stuck inside."

"Oh don't you worry, Mom." she said, as she whipped out a skinny bristled brush from her utensil drawer.

"You're kidding me, right? I would rather drink right out of the glass and forsake the straws. All this high maintenance stuff is going to shorten your life."

After I got home, I had to alert her of breaking news. The metal straws could be hazardous to your health. Someone poked a hole in her throat when she tripped and fell while drinking from a metal straw. Now, I don't remember the source, and whether this was fake news, but it certainly sounded possible to me. And I, with a history of falling, decided from that day forward to drink right out of a glass.

I do have a confession to make. I keep a box of disposable, plastic straws in the cabinet, but I use them only for the glass of water on my bedside table. They're bendable, so when I roll over in the middle of the night for a sip of water, I don't drown myself.

Our Losing Sickness

#

A few of our kids inherited from me the "losing phone, keys, and everything else sickness." And it's not just that we lose them, but we panic when we lose them. And sometimes we panic when we don't even lose them.

Let me explain. In the early part of our marriage, I would take my handbag into a restaurant, and sometimes while driving home with Paul would realize, as if I got struck by a bolt of lightning, that my purse was missing. After going into a convulsion and unlocking my seatbelt, with Paul nearly plowing into the car in front of us, I'd feel it next to me and say, "Oh, sorry about that. I found it." In my defense, it was dark.

After 50 years of marriage, he's now used to my purse panic and doesn't even twitch anymore.

It happens with my keys and phone, too. I wonder if I had that reaction when I lost a kid in Target. (I only did that once.)

I remember driving our daughter and her husband to the airport one time. Craig put the suitcases in the trunk, along with Eleanor's purse. Halfway to the airport, Craig got a devilish look in his eye and asked Eleanor if she had any mints in her purse, which was followed by a panicked seizure. They're still married.

I don't know why we get that initial adrenaline rush. If it happens when the girls and I are together, we all just smile. We probably need therapy for this disorder, but if it gives us something to laugh about, it's not worth the money.

Not all the losses create panic. I have gotten calls over the years from the YMCA in Rhode Island, a skating rink in Boston Commons, and a store asking if they were speaking to "Mom." Oh no—Sharon lost her phone again? Two of the times she didn't even know it was lost—just figured it was somewhere in the house.

Another time our son, Brian, called Sharon from his beach cottage. "Why is your phone in my freezer?"

"You found it!" shrieked a very ecstatic Sharon. "I must have laid it down in your freezer when I was getting ice pops for the kids yesterday."

When things are truly lost, our extrovert children have it on the family text thread within seconds. We say the prayer learned years ago. "Saint Anthony, Saint Anthony, please come around. Something is lost and cannot be found." Saint Anthony is really, really tired of hearing from the Hoyt family.

112

Japanese Beetles

For years I was very adamant about using *natural* methods to get rid of the Japanese beetles, which chomp on the leaves and petals of my Knock Out Roses every July. Twice a day, I was out in the front garden with my glass of water, spiked with lemon dish detergent. I picked them off my rose bushes with a vengeance and dropped them into the glass of soapy water that looked more like a Budweiser with a head of foam. It never occurred to me to explain what I was doing to the neighbors who stared at me on their morning walks. However, I never did get an AA pamphlet in my mailbox.

Well—I'm done with that. I picked off hundreds of beetles over the years, and they still kept coming back, mocking me for my efforts.

So—I bought a bottle of insecticide. I sprayed the bushes with the same vengeance I had when plucking the beetles. The next day, when I was sure I ruined not only the roses, but also the planet, I found the bush was blooming in all its glory, and not one Japanese beetle in sight.

And by the way, to protect the bees, I only use the insecticide on the rose bushes. All my other flowers will depend on the birds to slurp up unwanted petal chomping bugs. The bees must not be harmed. They are partners in my garden.

Too Many Choices

###

I have an issue with too many choices, which waste precious brain energy. I am speaking about the new light bulbs. I know they're supposed to save you money and last much longer (in my case, probably till I'm dead). But I need a tutorial every time I have to replace one of our old bulbs. I did research on Google before writing this so I wouldn't sound completely stupid, but I felt worse after reading some very lengthy articles about what used to be the lowly light bulb.

Did you know that the old-fashioned lightbulb we grew up with was called incandescent, and the lights under our kitchen cabinets were fluorescent? Yes? Well, me too.

But here's where it gets crazy. Now we have: CFL, LED, Halogen, and terms such as lumens, Light Kelvin Scale, and at the bottom of the list—watts! Oh give me back my watts—25 watts for romance, 40 for ambience with company, (unless you have a husband who says, "Please turn the lights up. I can't see a damn thing."), 60 watts to read, unless you are over 60—then you probably need 100 watts.

I'm now comfortable buying a light bulb. Even though there is more information than I care to know on the cardboard containers—if I bring my reading glasses, I can eventually find the words "replacement for a 60 watt bulb," hiding in all the scientific jargon.

Oh, I almost forgot. Do you want blue light or yellow? That's very important for reading at night. You don't want to affect your melatonin level.

And I thought picking out panty hose was such a dilemma in 1980!

Selling My Book

###

In the introduction I told you how I hated selling Girl Scout cookies, praying that no one would answer the door after I rang the bell.

I've come a long way since then, especially when it comes to selling my book, to the point of being irritating—like a mosquito, according to Paul. But, I learned that my book will go unread unless I market it. I surely didn't spend hours and days and months sitting in front of the computer, ignoring my dear husband and friends to have my words disappear into a black hole.

After the initial launch, I got an adrenalin rush with family and friends, and friends of friends buying my book. After that, I realized it's all up to me to keep my words relevant—which means, sadly, I am searching the Internet instead of writing. And on the web, I find voluminous tips along with marketers who are dying to help me out—for a fee.

I apologize to my Facebook friends for my book posts, but I try to be strategic, without being annoying—giving gentle reminders that the holidays are coming and it's a really easy gift to get your Aunt Matilda. You don't have to worry about her diabetes, as this gift doesn't have sugar; you don't have to know her size; if you get her the ebook, she can enlarge the print; and you won't add to her knickknack collections, which her children will thank you for, down the road.

I am happy if I solved your gift dilemma.

My marketing chutzpah has surprised even me. I was waiting on a bench for friends outside a Florida restaurant one day, when a couple came out and we got talking. It turns out they were from Delaware too, familiar with Rehoboth Beach. I told them how much I loved the area and mentioned that I belonged to the Rehoboth Beach Writers

Guild. Two minutes later, after I found out they liked to read humor, I handed them my card with the book information and off they went, thanking me profusely.

Another time, I was sitting in the waiting room after getting eye drops during one of my numerous pre-and-post cataract surgery appointments. The room was crowded (before the pandemic social distancing), and after 15 minutes of church-like quiet, someone brought up restaurants.

"Do you have a favorite fish place in the area?" he asked. All ears perked up and in the next 10 minutes I got the names of the best fish place, best Mexican, best Italian…

The room got quiet again. "Does anybody like to read humor?" I asked with a big grin. I guess they didn't expect that question. I sure didn't get the same response as the best place to eat crabs. I told them I wrote a book, and they all seemed impressed. Once more, the room got quiet.

And then from the far end of the room—"What was the name of that Italian place again?"

I had left my author business cards in the car that day. I'm sure if they saw the image of my book cover on the card, they would have raced home to order it on Amazon.

It helps to eavesdrop a bit when I am near a group of people, although Paul cringes, afraid I will turn into that irritating mosquito. I don't descend on just anyone. If they are middle to older age women, and they look like they are the lighthearted type that could relate to my stories, my fear of selling Girl Scout cookies becomes a distant memory.

Picking Out Paint Colors and Tile

###

I know what I like and I know what I don't like, when picking out paint or furniture for our home. But there's a huge gray area where my decision-making brain cells just laugh at me.

My last paint choice was a success, but that's because I taped fifty different color chips with variations of grayish-blue all over the walls. Morning, noon, and night, with different lighting, I studied them until my eyes started seeing purple.

"Make a decision, Mary Ann," pleaded Paul.

"I will, but I want the end result to be a subtle look—like a misty sky in Nantucket."

"You've never been to Nantucket."

My hesitation stemmed from past mistakes, when I went through a painting phase. In one of our previous homes, I wanted the color of our bedroom walls to coordinate with a new quilt that had navy blue and forest green squares, separated by thin yellow lines. I tried to match the yellow paint exactly to the shade in the fabric, and spent the next two years trying to convince myself that I loved the fluorescent pineapple yellow which blinded me with its psychedelic brightness when I opened my eyes every morning.

We lived for 26 years in New Jersey, while the kids were growing up, and decided to have ceramic tile installed in the kitchen and hallway of our home. I found a store that let me take tile samples and keep them for two days. They didn't realize I was planning to haul 25 of their heavy ceramic squares into the back of our car. We almost needed to replace the rear struts on our station wagon.

After moving the tiles around in the kitchen and hallway, Paul and I picked the winner. They were a peaceful combination of chocolate brown and cream—and they were shiny. Yes, I wanted *shiny* to replace the dull, over-waxed linoleum floors. And yes, they were a perfect choice—except for the shiny.

You see, with four kids, there were always puddles of melted snow or spilled soup on the floor. The Hoyts narrowly escaped broken bones and lawsuits from our visitors to 321 Ascot Lane.

I WANT AN AGENT!

#

Remember the good old days when a human voice answered if you called a business?

"Good afternoon, may I help you?"

"Yes, I have a problem with my clothes dryer."

"Let me direct you to someone who can help."

click

"Hello Ma'am. May I help you?"

"Yes, I am having a problem with my clothes dryer."

"Well, this is *parts*, Ma'am. What do you want me to order for you?"

"I have no idea! That's why I called."

"Let me switch you to someone who can help."

click

"Good afternoon, Ma'am. This is technical support. How may I help you?"

"Sir, I have a problem with my clothes dryer—and I am calling the mental health hotline if you connect me to one more department."

"Oh please, don't do that. How about I set up an appointment for a technician to come out."

Yes, those were the good old days.

Things haven't changed much, but at least back then you could share your frustrations with a human voice.

Now, when I call a business (let's say an insurance company), I get an automated voice that croons, "If you are an employer, press 1. If you are a customer, press 2."

Then, "Please tap in your 15 digit ID number followed by the pound key."

Then, "Ok, now press 1 for your account information; press 2 for pre-authorization; press 3 if you want to learn about a healthy options food plan."

"I want an agent!" I scream into the phone.

"I'm sorry. I didn't understand your choice."

"Of course you didn't understand my choice. I'm about to have a baby and my water broke and I'm out of state! I want to know which doctors are in my plan! And I want an agent before I slip and fall on my amniotic fluid!"

"Holy crap! Don't you think you should go to the hospital?" breaks in a human voice.

Oy vey.

By the way, I wasn't really having a baby. It just made the story better.

A Nurse's Story—Different Perspectives

###

Back in the days when I worked on a hospital medical-surgical floor, I read a nursing magazine article that suggested asking family members of elderly patients to bring in photographs from their younger, happier days to place on their bedside tables.

"What a great idea," I thought—an excellent reminder that our frail, gray-haired patients in hospital gowns did indeed have vibrant pasts.

I had a patient back then, with serious, chronic health problems who had frequent stays on our unit. Her day consisted of being on the receiving end of medications, lab tests, and IV fluids.

Remembering the magazine article, I asked the family, in front of the patient, if they had any pictures of their mom when she was young. They brought one in the next day, and I could hardly believe it was the same person. The stunning woman in the photo exuded self-assurance and happiness. The enthusiasm I expressed was sincere, for it helped me to see her life more in its entirety—an intimate glance into her past, showing a woman who raised a family, made decisions, laughed, and danced.

A week later, I noticed that the photo was sitting on the window sill on the far side of the room. And on her next admission to our unit, a month later, the picture did not accompany her.

While caring for her one day, the subject came up. Imagine my surprise when she hesitated, and then said, "I felt like I was at a funeral."

That perspective had never occurred to me, and I'm not sure my patient could have predicted her reaction. In retrospect, I remember feeling bad, but I learned that involving the patient and being sensitive to their needs may not always prevent a situation like this. Regarding the bedside photograph, I tend to believe her experience might be the exception.

I can see other patients getting a boost to their self-esteem, as they receive compliments and questions about the photo. What a precious tool for reminiscing, which is an old person's gift.

Photos are windows into someone's past. The nursing staff will be reminded daily that the baseball player in the windup stance on the pitcher's mound could be someone's dad, with a competitive spirit and a powerful pitching arm—preparing him for the challenges later in life.

Throw Pillows

###

OK—this is a fluffy, superficial piece, to help you decompress after my nurse's story.

I am not big on throw pillows. Or rather—I am a minimalist when it comes to them. I found a couple for our sofa that displayed understated elegance. And they're staying there forever.

It's not to say that I won't buy another pillow if I see something pretty and I feel like a change. I'm just not out on the hunt for the sake of change.

I feel the same way about throw pillows on my bed. When all I want to do is jump into bed because I am bone-tired (even though I'll be wide awake when I'm horizontal), the last thing I want to do is remove a ton of throw pillows that are just there for show. And—where to put them? I can't get myself to throw them on the floor, because in nursing school, we were told NOTHING was allowed on the floor but our feet; so the two extra pillows get thrown onto the only chair in our bedroom.

And to all our friends, who have hosted us overnight—if you can't find your throw pillows in the guest bedroom after we leave (which were quite lovely, by the way), just look in your closet. I probably forgot to put them back on the bed.

And that's the end of my short fluffy piece.

Birds

###

One day Sharon, our oldest, was talking about how birds have always freaked her out. And it's not liked she ever watched Alfred Hitchcock's *The Birds*.

"I gave you a calendar with paintings of colorful song birds last year at Christmas. I would have given you the one with sunsets if I knew that." I hate to fail with a Christmas present, especially one that I spent an hour in Hallmark to find the perfect meaningful calendar.

With the exception of humming birds (they scare me), I really do like birds. Oh, wait a minute. I forgot one other bird that scares me—the swooping swallow. I had to Google why birds were dive-bombing me while I was on a walk one day. Apparently the swallows just wanted to protect their little baby birdies in the nearby nests by scaring me away. I'm telling you—walking is dangerous.

Speaking of nests, we came home from Florida at the end of March one year to find a nest in our front door wreath. My neighbor told me the noisy little bird sitting on the sky blue eggs was a house wren. We missed the hatching of the babies, but watched them stick their tiny beaks into the air each day, waiting for food. The most fascinating spectacle to watch was on the day they flew out of the nest to the grass a few yards away. How the heck did they know how to fly? I don't know what I was expecting, but was sure the mother would give them a lesson or two.

The aftermath—what a mess. I never really noticed because I had everyone use the garage door while we had a bird nursery on our front door. Bird poop was everywhere—in the nest, on the side of the nest, on my wreath, down the front door, and on the welcome mat. I didn't even try to save my pretty winter wreath with puffs of fake snow and pinecones.

I thought this was a onetime event, but a noisy little house wren did the same thing the next year. I wondered if it was the same bird who happened to like its previous accommodations. I need to up her rent to cover the new wreath and the annual cleaning expenses.

One last bird reference is a 40-year-old memory. Every spring they used to wake up my babies and toddlers at 5:30 in the morning with their incessant chirping and twittering. It was like the Boston Pops outside. It didn't matter if the windows were open or closed. I never did forgive them for that.

So, again—why do I like birds?

No—I Did Not Steal the Chicken

###

I can be a bit flighty at times. I remember going to help our daughter-in-law who was on bedrest, years ago, because of a problem during her pregnancy. She and our son were only married a couple of years, and I was still learning the ropes of how to be a good mother-in-law.

I did some food shopping at a nearby Trader Joe's, and figured I'd throw in a couple of magazines to help her pass the time. The next day, when I asked her if she got any juicy gossip from them, she smiled and told me she did—from *Us Weekly*. Apparently I bought the Spanish version of *People Magazine*.

I know you are wondering what this has to do with stealing a chicken. I'm getting there.

My biggest "flighty" fear is that I will absentmindedly run out of a store with something I forgot to pay for, while talking to a friend on my iPhone's AirPods. Now, I am very honest. More than once, I've gone back into the grocery store to pay for a box of toothpicks or a birthday card that I found in the bottom of the grocery cart while loading the car. I've got the supermarket's badge of honesty.

Anyway, my reputation almost got completely unraveled the other day in the self-checkout aisle. I had my pandemic mask on. Either I suffered from a lack of oxygen, or I was pre-occupied—deciding whether I should make one more stop in my search for a flat iron steak. Halfway through checking out, the employee who was monitoring the self-checkout registers came up behind me and said, "Ma'am, you put that chicken in the bag without scanning it." The blood went to my feet.

"I am so sorry. I have never done that before," I replied, my voice shaking. My hands were shaking too, as I pulled the 8 pound chicken from the bag to scan it. Did she believe me? Did she remember that

I'm the one who brought back the box of toothpicks which I found in the bottom of my cart? With her mask on, I couldn't tell by her eyes. All I know was that she stood nearby, as I continued to scan my items.

I wondered if I would now have a rap sheet at the grocery store. On the way out, I repeated my apology, to which she replied, "Things happen."

I needed to do a better job of diffusing the situation. So I added, "Please don't tell my children. They might put me in a home." Finally, I could imagine a smile under her mask. And I know she believed me.

Mary Ann

###

When I was about four or five, there was a popular song composed by Rafael de Leon that went: "Down by the sea shore, Mary Ann; down by the sea shore, sifting sand."

And then in the 60s, the Four Seasons "C'mon Marianne," topped the charts. Being a teenager at the time, it was a big deal to hear my name played over and over on the radio. I was sure that handsome heads were turning every time the song came on.

Interestingly, I never had a hurricane named after me. The closest I came was Hurricane Marilyn in 1995 and Hurricane Maria in 2017.

I am not even on the future list of names that the World Meteorological Organization picked out for hurricanes that are still twinkles in the eye of the universe. Yep, they are already chosen—must have been a slow day at the office.

I ought to be thankful for this omission. Whenever the name of a certain deadly hurricane comes up in conversation, I feel bad for the Katrinas of the world.

I would rather be remembered for sifting sand.

Seconds

I come from a family that loves to eat. My mother made the best fried chicken and Hungarian dishes that she learned from her mother-in-law—simmered in sour cream, onions, and paprika. Molasses cookies or gingerbread would be sitting on the kitchen table when we came home from school. Even my dad used to cook. He was so proud of his chili and creamed cucumbers.

My father worked at the Bethlehem Steel and times were tough during the steel strikes, but we never wanted for food. And we didn't have dainty portions on our plates, either. In fact, after we all finished dinner, my mother would say, "Okay, who wants seconds?" It was a given that we all did.

Surprisingly, we were not obese. Of course, those were the days when we worked it off outside, at a playground three blocks away. The little borough that was home to us was called Fountain Hill, and we had plenty of hills to stretch our hamstrings.

There was one perplexing thing I noticed when our girls brought their boyfriends home for dinner. Each guy, on different occasions, would respond to my question, "How about a second helping?" with, "No thanks. It was really good, Mrs. Hoyt. But I've had plenty."

Our daughters are all married now, to these self-disciplined guys. And, to their chagrin, their husbands still stop at one helping most of the time. I always thought the male species had insatiable appetites. I know our family does, and gender has nothing to do with it.

I take hydration and nutrition seriously. We had very few incidents of high fevers in our house. The second the kids' temperatures went over 98.6, I'd get into my *feed a cold, starve a fever* mode. Their tummies were full of chicken soup, ginger ale, and toast before the Tylenol had a chance to reach the hypothalamus in their brains.

Mealtime has definitely been good for our marriage. My mother, a 1950s wife, used to tell me, "The way to a man's heart is through his stomach." I found it to be true.

When we were first married, Paul was a picky eater. As a bachelor, he lived on steak, cheeseburgers and his home-made, specialty meatloaf (with which he couldn't wait to dazzle me).

I remember asking him, after we got back from our honeymoon, "How about Hungarian goulash for dinner?"

"I don't eat that."

"What do you mean, you don't eat that? Have you ever tried it?"

"No, but I'd rather have something else."

The second time I asked about chicken paprikash and got a similar answer. I thought, "Screw this! I'm not asking him anymore. I love cooking, and he's not going to rain on my parade in the kitchen!"

So, I stopped asking and started making all kinds of dinners, some that I learned from my mother, and others that were experiments. And surprise—my hungry man likes 98 percent of my concoctions. And the best part is when he asks for seconds!

Breaking News

Most of my friends know I'm a news junkie. I think I got the nose for news from my father. Even though he didn't attend college, you would never know it by the content of our dinner conversations. He read the *Bethlehem Globe Times* and the *New York Daily News* from beginning to end. My dad died before cable news became popular, but I picked up the slack. In fact, I can't wait to tune in first thing in the morning to hear what happened on the other side of the world while America was sleeping.

If it wasn't for the caffeine in my coffee, I would just crawl back into bed after listening to the glut of unnerving stories. I can easily get sucked into the 24-hour news cycle, but I devised a strategy so I can get on with my life.

I mute the TV. In the beginning of this muting trial, I would put the sound back on when I saw the words *Breaking News* pop up in the lower left-hand corner of the screen. Until I finally realized, it says *Breaking News* almost all the time. Ha! You shrewd, scheming producers.

I'm getting better at determining when there's a real crisis. It's all about the facial expressions of the commentators—oh, and flames. Flames are always bad.

When I'm at the computer, like I am now working on my book, I sneak over to the Internet ever so infrequently (ha!) to check my mail. On my home page what do I see but an update on my state of Delaware regarding the virus, and a tornado watch in our area. After that, the rest is just gossip, which I also can't resist—like when I got the urge to see what Robert Redford looks like today. Well, these shysters now have a "Next page" trick. I have to click through 40 pages of actors before I can see Robert Redford. So, whenever "Next page" pops up, I go back to writing my book. Serves me right for wasting time.

I need to take a break now, because it's almost time for dinner and the Nightly News.

Insomnia

###

Menopause, for me, has been pretty much a breeze. Paul would probably disagree. I can't say I'm any more emotionally unstable than I usually am, and I escaped the hot flashes that wake up many women during the night in a pool of sweat.

I do have one symptom from this dearth of hormones, though—insomnia. It's not painful or uncomfortable—just annoying.

Is my insomnia caused by the hot shower I take before bed which is supposed to relax me? Is it my last Facebook check?

Reading is supposed to help. However, as my eye lids begin to droop and I place my ebook on the bedside table, the second I scrooch into the fetal position, I'm wide awake.

I don't even drink anything at night with caffeine, a common culprit. I may have gotten a clue from my sister-in-law, who always had coffee in the evening. She said that coffee never kept her up. An unresolved issue did.

Well, maybe I solved the puzzle. I always have unresolved issues.

Do I want to be buried or cremated? Time's running out. How awful to leave that decision to the kids.

Speaking of the kids, I have to get down to the basement to get rid of *stuff* before we move again, or die.

What book title should I give this book? How is it I can write a whole book, but I can't come up with ten words for a title?

And speaking of books, I could check my first book's *Amazon Best Selling Rank* on my iPhone (if you purchase one, my rank will go up and you'll help me sleep better). Oh wait, if you are reading this, I guess you already did. Thank you.

And— I need to make a mental note to call Verizon tomorrow and find out why my phone keeps saying the storage is full. What do I need to delete? Of course, since I can't sleep, maybe I could delete emails that go all the way back to 2005. But that would mean I'd have to open each one up to see why I thought I needed to save it in the first place.

No, I'm too tired for that kind of a project.

I think I'll drag myself into the computer room and write a few more words for this book, after eating a handful of chips.

30 minutes later
Good night.

Future Nurse?

###

One of our granddaughters thinks she wants to be a nurse someday. If she ends up following her dream, she'll have lots of first-hand experience because of her numerous visits to the local hospital's emergency room. Eleanor, her mother, is so squeamish, she can barely look at someone's arm in a cast. She usually sits in the ER with her eyes in a squint the whole time so she doesn't faint.

Her daughter, on the other hand, has her eyeballs wide open, taking everything in. The CT scan to rule out appendicitis—WOW! An IV insertion into her arm—"Can I watch?" A patient howling in the next cubicle, as Eleanor turns pale—"Do you think if I ask, they'll tell me what's wrong with him?"

"No honey, they have privacy rules."

This future nurse is delighted if they leave the curtain open a tad in front of her cubicle, so she can stare at the gurneys flying by with oxygen masks on faces and hopefully a little blood.

Her concussion from doing flips when clowning around with friends the year before wasn't a good thing. But I guess it will help with the *concussion protocol* on her neurology exam someday.

I need to give her fair warning, though, that it's not always exciting and dreamy. It's very hard work, even if you are not in the Intensive Care Unit, and you never get completely used to the smells and some of the unpleasant visuals. But, surprisingly, one sign that you are nurse material is that despite all the blood and gore, you can still down a slice of pizza for lunch.

Ebooks and Shopping Online

I'm sure I love my ebook for the same reasons that most people like theirs. However, I used to be one of those serious readers who said, a bit haughtily, "I much prefer reading a book the old-fashioned way. The smell of the pages in a book just off the presses, or the slightly musty smell of a vintage treasure is mesmerizing to my senses."

Well, all that's true, but now that I have the eyes of a 90-year-old, my tune has changed. It's not just that you can enlarge the print on an ebook—you can also make the backlight brighter. One of our kids, looking over my shoulder at the beach as I was reading asked, "You sure you've got the print large enough, Mom? I could read that page up at the snack bar."

"Yea, honey, just you wait."

I no longer have to balance a heavy book (with its attached book light) in bed next to my sleeping husband. No, I just turn the pages of my light weight ebook with the tap of a finger.

The tap of a finger also works pretty well when I shop—on the computer. Once I found out how easy it was to click on Amazon and buy my computer's printer ink, or Paul's Nike gym socks, I was hooked. One tap of the finger on the site that has all my information and I get a message, "Your order will arrive in two days."

"You know, we need to keep track of this stuff that keeps showing up at our front door, and how much is accumulating on our credit card," says you know who.

Now, when it comes to my clothes, I still go into a store so I can feel the fabric and look in the mirror after I try it on. I never trust to my imagination what I see on the hanger.

Oh, and by the way, you think it's funny that I need to feel the fabric? Next time you're in Target or Stein Mart, observe how all the women caress the dresses as they go up and down the aisles. We don't even realize we're doing it.

Paul's Radical Prostate Surgery

###

A few weeks after we were married, Paul got a cold. "Honey, you couldn't be in a better place. I will use all my nursing knowledge to get you through this."

And then I realized, I was more equipped to care for someone with a heart ailment or a fracture than an adult male with a cold. To be kind, he does get these weird colds where it looks like he's crying—tears dripping from his eyes, that antihistamines don't help very much.

"Maybe you should take my temperature. I think I have a fever," he informs me.

Then comes the soup, the cold medicine, the cough drops, the reassurance...

"Can't you just hibernate in your bedroom 'til this is over?" I asked on the third day?

"I hope this isn't how you talk to your patients in the hospital," he said between sneezes.

I dreaded the thought of him ever getting a serious diagnosis and being really sick. I will need back-up, I thought.

And then he got the serious diagnosis—prostate cancer in 2010. That "C" word has a way of turning your lives upside down. We made an appointment for a second opinion. Not being very internet savvy back then, I bought a copy of Dr. Patrick Walsh's *Guide to Surviving Prostate Cancer*. I poured over every word written by the Johns Hopkins' expert in urology, leaving yellow sticky notes on pages I wanted to read out loud to Paul.

He ended up having a radical prostatectomy, followed by radiation a few months later. Even though he had an aggressive form of prostate cancer, he is free from this disease ten years later.

But the other thing I wanted to tell you—I didn't need back-up. Paul was a real trouper. He handled the post-op pain well, thanked me for everything I did, and hardly ever complained. Maybe there is some psychology in knowing you got your life back.

Last week he had one of his colds, with the teary eyes, the sneezing, the cough drops, the reassurance. I won't complain.

My Admiration of Free Verse Poetry

Back in the '50s, our poetry lessons consisted mostly of poems that rhymed. Also, remember the term iambic pentameter? It's a rhythmic pattern that I still can't explain.

Today, many poets write *free verse* poetry. To me the writing seems like prose with fewer words. It flows to its own rhythm—free from constraints and extraneous sounds. I see beauty in the raw substance of its images. And, after reading it, I always think somebody really smart wrote it, or that maybe, somebody wrote it who wants to *sound* really smart.

I wonder why writing free verse poetry intimidates me. I think the words in my brain want rules, a predictable rhythm, and they like it if I can make them rhyme. Although, come to think of it, *McCall's* magazine rejected the sing-songy poem I wrote when I was 12. And my rhyming skills didn't improve much since then.

I consulted my old friend, Google, to see if a certain brain skill was needed to write free verse, but found nothing helpful.

I should ask Brian, our son, who is a good writer. He often waxes poetic, with long free verse poems in birthday cards to me, or in Facebook posts about world events.

"What's he trying to say?" asked my husband, after a recent post.

"Read it again and think about the meaning, honey. Although, on second thought, why don't you just call him."

Little White Lies

We teach our children not to lie. Sometimes, I tell a little white lie, or a fib. They're not as bad, right? Like when I went for my pre-cataract surgery visit. I wasn't honest when they asked me how much I weigh. I figured if I got to my target weight by the day of surgery, it was no longer a lie.

And you can't tell me you've never given compliments that were flattering but untrue. I get around telling the whole truth on Facebook by just clicking "like" on a new hairdo post. Or, if I'm really honest, I don't do anything. They'll just figure I never saw it.

Then there are the husband fibs. For example, sometimes Paul is on a need to know basis. And that's to save him from high blood pressure or worse. Why did he need to know about the near collision when I drove down a one way street the wrong way. I refuse to burden him with things like that.

And the time I cleaned out the garage when he was on a business trip many years ago—getting rid of stuff he would probably hang onto forever, just in case. I took the chance that he wouldn't miss the rusty, old fishing reel and odd- looking widgets with dangling wires I couldn't identify—all sent to their graveyard in the dump. On his return, he was elated that he could finally get through our tiny garage without breaking an ankle. And his work bench—how did it get so neat?

"Honey, the neatness fairy must have organized your stuff!" He never missed a thing.

My Husband's Cure for Everything—Exercise

###

Me: "Why am I so sleepy today?"
Paul: "Why don't you get out and get some exercise."

Me: "I'm feeling anxious."
Paul: "You need to go for a walk."

Me: "My joints are so stiff today. I need to take some ibuprofen."
Paul: "Sounds like you need to stretch."

Me: "I think I'm pregnant."
Paul: "You're what???"
Me: "Just kidding."

It's hard being married to a jock. I think he did calisthenics in his mother's womb, and hasn't missed a day of exercise since. And there's nothing he can't do. He's played football, tennis, handball, softball, and golf. He ran in 6K races, threw a shotput, and in his spare time—went to the gym, which he does to this day.

He's right about the benefits of exercise, and I'm very proud of myself when I get back from a long walk (long being relative). But geez, it's like having Paul, my exercise angel on one shoulder and the lazy devil on the other, and they're in constant competition. In the summer, if I don't get out of the house before 10, the exercise angel is out of luck. It just gets too hot in Delaware.

"How about I get you a gym membership, Mary Ann," suggests my Tiger Woods.

"Honey, I will take that under advisement."

Car Seats

###

Birthing children when you're young isn't just about healthy sperm and eggs. It's also about the healthy shoulders, hips, and knees of the mother. Not sure if my joints would have survived four kids if I had to use today's regulation safety baby and child car seats.

In the early '70s, we put the top part of the old-fashioned baby carriage on the back seat and let the baby roll around under a blanket and bounce herself to sleep. When they graduated to a child's car seat, they sat in a flimsy, elevated seat with a handle bar in front of them; and if they were lucky, they even had a little tray table piled with Cheerios.

When the kids were too big to fit in the seat, they got thrown into the back of our station wagon. They learned to pad the tailgate with their coats to break the impact from my sudden accelerations.

What a shock when I took our first grandbaby for a ride in my car. "Mom," called Sharon from the kitchen. "I left the baby car seat by the front door." I felt pretty smart that I knew it had to go in the back seat, and face to the rear—which still seems absolutely crazy to me. The infant's sight is developing and all the baby gets to see is dull gray car upholstery. That's mean.

Now, which seatbelt goes under this thing and which strap goes where. As I emerged from the car in a sweat, Sharon was approaching with her 5- month-old bundle of smiles. Sharon peeked into the car. She handed the baby to me and reached in to give the car seat the wiggle test.

"Mom, you didn't do a very good job of installing this. The baby and the car seat will be on the floor when you make your first stop. Here, let me redo this." Now I lost my confidence, and after I placed the little treasure in the seat, my trembling hands tried to slip her pudgy arms under the car seat straps and snap the clasp.

"You don't think it's too tight, do you?" I asked as I was checking that her fingertips were still pink.

"She's fine, Mom. Just do me a favor. When you come back, call me on my cell, so I can come and help you get her out."

So off we went. Three times I stopped the car and got out to check for breathing and circulation, and each time she smiled at me. This was a lot of work for a 15-minute ride around the neighborhood.

When they graduated to *child* car seats, we bought our own, so we didn't have to keep taking it in and out of the car. The directions that were pages long, came with straps and clasps and widgets. In desperation I went to the local fire department, which was promoting car safety and offering free help installing child car seats.

Securing a wiry toddler into this straight jacket was a whole new ball game. I made sure another adult was within screaming distance in case I fell into the kid and started to suffocate him; or in case I needed the rescue squad and their Jaws of Life to extract me in the event my joints froze.

I developed a new respect for our adult children who were up to this task. The years flew by fast—no more car seats and our grandkids now put on their own seatbelts.

We like to help out when we visit by driving the grandchildren to their sports practices when the parents are at work. The kids all looked puzzled when I turned on my GPS for a three mile trip.

"We know the way, Grandma."

"I know. It's just in case you forget to look up from your iPhones."

I still don't know why they complain of headaches after I get to the field. They probably need to drink more water.

"Who's driving me to soccer practice today?" asked a granddaughter on our last visit.

"Granddad is," said her mother, and I heard a sigh of relief.

The Silver Lining

#

I am officially a homebody. The pandemic made that very clear to me. In fact, my daughter told me I've been practicing for a pandemic my whole life. It's not that I don't like to party and travel, but I also never realized how much I like my solitude.

And of course, writing a book demands many solitary hours in a chair—typing and revising. To be honest, though, I'm lucky if I get two hours in front of the computer each day.

There's really no excuse for that during a pandemic when I am sheltering in place. I'm just not disciplined enough to get up at dawn and bring my coffee into our computer room to write, like I imagine the great authors do. My mind isn't clear enough to create until after the breakfast dishes are in the dishwasher, my roses are dead-headed, the washing machine's humming in the laundry room, and my power walk (ha) is done. Even though it's the afternoon by now, I'm happy as a lark, ready to type away.

The coronavirus hasn't come to our doorstep (at least not as this book goes to print), so I am very, very grateful.

I have felt so relaxed, not feeling pressure to go anywhere. Once a week grocery shopping replaced my daily stop for whatever I forgot to buy the day before. Paul was about to stick a surveillance camera on my car, because nobody could possibly like going to the supermarket that much.

The sheltering in place had a silver lining for me. While I love the beach, (and the Atlantic Ocean is only 25 minutes from us), if I was in the middle of writing a chapter, during the lockdown phase, I no longer had to pop up and go with surfer boy. Not that I don't like hanging out with my sweetheart on the sand, but I can be just as happy typing with the breeze blowing through the window while Paul (my artiste!) is creating on canvas another nautical oil painting.

With the hiatus on live sports events, we started binge watching a few TV series together in the evening. Our kids found it amusing when they called, and I texted back, "Daddy and I are watching an episode of *The Marvelous Mrs Maisel*. We'll call you back."

And for the first time ever, I got the chance to see my garden flowers grow, as if I was watching time lapse photography. Sitting on my rocker outside, I've watched the butterflies travel from my Shasta daisies to the hydrangeas and back again. Unaware of my presence, a goldfinch pecked at the seeds of my black-eyed Susans, while two perky little squirrels got into a scuffle out on the lawn.

Should I be enjoying this pandemic silver lining when so many families are ripped apart because of this nasty virus without a cure? The mental anguish so many are going through, along with the struggle to put food on the table and educate their children saddens me.

When my mind drifts off to these realities, I pray. I don't feel so helpless then. I call our kids and grandchildren. I try to be a good listener. I watch *The Crown* on TV in the evening with my dear husband.

And I keep writing. I hope I made you smile.

The End

Acknowledgments

I am indebted to those who read my rough drafts which were full of thoughts, observations, and memories. They had the patience and skill to give me suggestions, find my errors, and help me polish my potpourri of words. As they were reading the humorous pieces, I appreciated their honesty when they tactfully encouraged me to use funnier words. So—a big thank you to Cindy Hall and Linda Federman of the Rehoboth Beach Writers Guild, and Stephanie Hoyt, my daughter-in-law.

I also want to thank Maribeth Fischer, Executive Director of the Rehoboth Beach Writers Guild for her encouragement, and also, the members of our weekly writers chat group.

Regarding my husband, I want to thank him for all his helpful suggestions, and I need to repeat what I said in the acknowledgments of my last book. Without the good nature of Paul, who winced every time I mentioned him in an anecdote, I could not have written this book. His faith in me made me believe I could do this a second time. I love you, Paul.

To my four dear children and their spouses, my grandchildren, my siblings, and my friends who all contributed in some way to this book, either by listening, giving me fodder to write about, or cheering me on—thank you.

Also by Mary Ann Hoyt

###

*In Heaven There's No Money, No Stuff—and No Porta-Potties
Coping With Life's Aggravations By Finding the Funny*